# DEDICATION

I dedicate this book to my grandmother Louise Haywood and my mother Deborah Polite, from whom I learned how to stand on my own two feet and get back on them when I get knocked down, make good choices, be humble, give thanks to God and to the people who have helped me along the way, and appreciate the finer things in life.

DEDICATION

# DIVAS DOING BUSINESS

---

## What the Guidebooks Don't Tell You
## About Being a Woman Entrepreneur

---

## MONIQUE HAYWARD

*Foreword by Morgan Freeman*

## Divas Doing Business
### What the Guidebooks Don't Tell You About Being a Woman Entrepreneur

ISBN: 978-0-615-26873-6

Editing: Laura Mariani
Table of Contents: Julie Kawabata
Cover and Interior Design and production: Studio 6 Sense • www.6sense.net

# ACKNOWLEDGEMENTS

To my husband Tom Freeman, the love of my life and an honorable, patient man who believes in my dreams, commits to being a partner in my success, takes the good with the bad, and gives me strength and confidence to take risks knowing he'll be there to catch me when I fall.

To my dear friends and family who support me emotionally, spiritually, and financially; encourage me to keep my dreams alive; and advise me on many matters, both large and small.

# CONTENTS

**Foreword by Morgan Freeman**..................................**11**

**Preface** .................................................................**15**

**Chapter 1: Am I Ready for This?**
*Your entrepreneurial journey is a balancing act.* ..................**17**

Divas Lesson #1: Define balance for yourself and
prepare for your entrepreneurial journey. ................................20

Preparing for the Journey: Q&A with **Pegine Echevarria**
Professional Success Coach, Motivational Speaker,
and Author..........................................................................24

**Chapter 2: Bringing the Dream to Life**
*Every idea begins with inspiration.* ...............................**33**

Divas Lesson #2: When seeking inspiration, leave no
stone unturned. Inspiration is all around you. .........................37

Inspiration: Q&A with **Lisa Price**
Carol's Daughter..................................................................38

**Chapter 3: The Business Plan is Your Holy Book**
*Write it yourself.* ...................................................**43**

Divas Lesson #3: Don't let someone else's
words speak for you. ...........................................................48

Business Plan: Q&A with **Margaret Wallace**
Rebel Monkey......................................................................49

## Chapter 4: The Real Deal on Raising Money
*Nobody just writes checks.* .......................................**55**

Divas Lesson #4: When it comes to money,
you will be able to figure it out. .................................... 64

Raising Money: Q&A with **Denise Brosseau**
Invent Your Future Enterprises.................................... 68


## Chapter 5: Hiring Rock Stars
*Your staff is your front line.* .....................................**75**

Divas Lesson #5: Find the rock stars
who will play your song. ............................................ 85

Hiring Rock Stars: Q&A with **Sondra Bernstein**
the girl & the fig restaurant...................................... 86


## Chapter 6: Marketing the Business
*Become a fearless promoter.* .....................................**91**

Divas Lesson #6: Be fearless when it
comes to promoting your business. ........................... 98

Marketing: Q&A with **Sheril Cohen Kunz**
Girl on the Go! ...................................................... 101


## Chapter 7: The Art of Networking
*Get to the right people.* .....................................**109**

Divas Lesson #7: It's not just who you know;
it's who they are. .................................................. 114

Networking: Q&A with **Crystal McCrary Anthony**
Lawyer, Novelist, Film/TV Producer, and Commentator...................... 115

## Chapter 8: Kindness and Compassion Have a Place in Business

*Giving back.* ...........................................................**121**

*Divas Lesson #8: Be kind and compassionate and more business will come your way.* ............................. 126

Kindness and Compassion: Q&A with **Valerie Red-Horse**
Red-Horse Native Productions and Tribal Finance/Asset Management for Western International Securities, Inc. ............................. 127

## Chapter 9: The Value of Making Mistakes

*Learning is a lifelong pursuit.* ...........................................**133**

*Divas Lesson #9: I live, I learn, I move on.* ............................. 136

Learning from Mistakes: Q&A with **Jacqueline Rhinehart**
Organic Soul Marketing ............................. 137

## Chapter 10: Bringing It Home

*The last word.* ...........................................................**141**

*Divas Lesson #10: Every day your business is open is a day you defy the odds.* ............................. 146

## About the Author ...........................................................**147**

## Endnotes ...........................................................**149**

## Appendices

A: Sample Business Plan ............................. 151

B: Marketing Plan Outline ............................. 187

# FOREWORD

I admire and respect smart, hardworking, enterprising women. Growing up in the segregated South in the heart of the Mississippi Delta in the 1940s and 1950s, I was surrounded by strong women – my mother, grandmother, aunts, teachers – who shaped my outlook on life, encouraged my moviemaking dreams despite the obstacles facing young black men, and taught me lessons that still guide me today. Throughout my multi-faceted career, I've worked with many women whose stories inspire me. Drive and ambition tend to attract me, and these women's dedication and commitment to their own success and that of others amaze me. My friend Monique Hayward stands out in these respects.

Monique excelled academically, graduating *magna cum laude* and Phi Beta Kappa in journalism from the University of Maryland College Park. She went on to get an MBA in marketing from Case Western Reserve University and launched a successful career in Corporate America in marketing, public relations, communications, and business development for high-tech companies. She has performed various assignments that have taken her around the world and has worked with prominent journalists, business leaders, government officials, and Hollywood celebrities.

Impressive? Yes. Enough for Monique? Absolutely not.

She decided to push herself further by putting her skills and knowledge into her own start-up business. Monique created Dessert Noir Café & Bar out of a personal desire and a growing market need to provide suburban diners with an upscale restaurant close to home, something to which I can completely relate with my own establishments, Madidi Restaurant in Clarksdale, Mississippi and Ground Zero Blues Club in Clarksdale and Memphis, Tennessee. Knowing the struggles of running a restaurant business and having dined at Dessert Noir Café & Bar myself, I have seen firsthand how Monique puts her heart and soul into her business. I can appreciate the challenges and opportunities Monique addresses every day to run her restaurant while pursuing her corporate career.

What I admire most about Monique is that while she may be tested time and again with balancing all the demands of her life, she never forgets to give back. Realizing my involvement in relief for hurricane victims, Monique approached me with a creative, out-of-the-box idea to involve her business and the local community in a multi-faceted celebrity charity event to assist me with raising funds for PLAN!T NOW, which empowers people with information they need to help protect their families, lives, homes, and businesses in the event of natural disasters. She's also assisted local non-profit organizations, schools, and charities with fundraising events and donations. There is also an interesting story about her giving a guy on a downtown Atlanta street who was down on his luck money for dinner and a bus ticket! That's how Monique is: If she's in a position to help, you can count on her to be there for you.

And that's what Monique has set out to do with this book. She wants to be right alongside you to share her knowledge and insight as you travel on your own entrepreneurial journey. Monique writes *Divas Doing Business* with a style that is direct, provocative, honest, and straightforward because she knows you need the straight story as you make critical decisions about starting and managing your business.

Monique has boundless energy, which means she's already working on what's next for herself and her business. Believe me: This is not last word you'll hear from her. She's just beginning.

Morgan Freeman

# PREFACE

*Divas Doing Business* came to me in one of those "the-last-straw-is-breaking-the-camel's-back moments" in early November 2006. My entire life seemed to be falling apart. My money-losing restaurant was creating extreme financial problems for me, including a multi-thousand-dollar lawsuit that jeopardized my credit rating and threatened my ability to secure additional financing. I had no good solutions for how to fix the mess I was in. My executive chef/general manager was in the throes of serious personal and family issues that were affecting his ability to focus on running the restaurant. My husband, who had displayed the patience of Job and supported me through both good times and bad, was at his wit's end and was ordering me to shut my business down. The demands of my day job at Intel Corporation were mounting as the company announced a major restructuring initiative that resulted in workforce reductions. I was laying off employees on my team, managing performance issues with those who remained, and taking on more responsibilities after our group fell into line with the rest of the company to do our jobs with fewer resources. I could hardly sleep or eat and my stress levels were off the chart. I cried and cried and cried...

Then one rainy night when I was all alone in my bedroom, I knelt at the side of my bed like I did when I was a little girl and prayed to God:

*"Dear God, what is my purpose in going through all of this turmoil and pain? What else can I do to have peace of mind and put my business on the path for success? What is it that you want me to do? Please show me the way and give me the strength to navigate the course You have charted for me."*

It took a few days of soul searching, praying, deep strategic thinking, and reflecting before it came to me: I know how to write and I know how to talk! Therefore, I'm obligated to bring you, my fellow "divas doing business," the story behind the story of being a woman entrepreneur, one of courage, hope, purpose, and undying commitment to success for all women who dare to pursue their dream of entrepreneurship.

This book is intended to be a straight-talking supplement to traditional how-to guides, providing insight into those business situations that will test your resolve, your strength, and your spirit in the real world. You will meet successful women entrepreneurs just like you who started in business with a great idea, a gut feeling, or a vision to deliver a product or service to the market and are now making their mark by inventing breakthroughs, rising above their competitors, commanding the respect of their peers, and pioneering important business and social trends.

We are in this together. Divas, hear me...

**CHAPTER 1**

# AM I READY FOR THIS?

### YOUR ENTREPRENEURIAL JOURNEY IS A BALANCING ACT.

## WOMEN BUSINESSES ARE HOT, BUT ARE THEY WORTH THE HEAT?

Throughout history, women have always sparked social, economic, and cultural trends and movements. As more of us pursue entrepreneurship, industry pundits, business writers, consultants, experts, and commentators declare that there is no better time than right now for women to be in business. They observe and report how we are redefining the business landscape on our own terms: "Women entrepreneurs ARE the trend," according to Susan Hadary, the former executive director of the Center for Women's Business Research. "Women business owners are changing the face of business, both literally and figuratively. The dynamic growth and expansion of women-owned businesses is one of the defining trends of the past decade, and all indications are that it will continue unabated." [1]

With that, the face of women's entrepreneurship is also changing as more women of color enter the arena. According to the Center for Women's Business Research's report titled *Businesses Owned by Women of Color in the United States 2008,* businesses owned by African-American, Asian, and Hispanic women substantially outpace all U.S. firms in revenue growth and number of employees.

Between 2002 and 2008, the number of privately-held firms 50 percent or more owned by women of color grew 30 percent while all other businesses grew nine percent. At the same time, revenues for these businesses grew 35 percent compared to 15 percent for all other firms. Employment also grew 22 percent compared to two percent for all firms. Women of color now represent 26 percent of all women business owners, up from 20 percent just a few years ago, and account for 2.3 million firms, 1.7 million jobs, and $235 billion in revenues.[2]

Conventional wisdom points to a bright future and preaches that if you have what it takes to be your own boss, follow the step-by-step process to turn your idea into a viable business, and work your plan, success for your small business should be well within your reach. However, according to the U.S. Small Business Administration (SBA), two-thirds of new small businesses survive at least two years, 44 percent at least four years, and 31 percent at least seven years.[3] You may be thinking to yourself, "Dynamic growth and expansion? Whoa! I can get better odds of winning on the slots in Las Vegas."

Well, there is definitely wisdom in the cliché, "If it was easy, everyone would be doing it." Entrepreneurs will get straight to the point when you ask them: Starting a business is difficult and risky and not for the faint of heart. Running your own company means you are responsible for everything in the operation, and at the end of the day, you are the "throat to choke," particularly during the start-up phase. As you get up and running and start to find your groove, you will become synonymous with your business, making it the top priority in your life whether you like it or not.

In general, embarking on the journey to start your own business is a challenging endeavor. Additionally, women entrepreneurs face unique circumstances and obstacles that can extend and complicate their journey and must leap over many hurdles to get access to capital, work harder to overcome the perception that a woman-owned business is not a high-growth opportunity, or constantly justify your existence to "good old boys" with the power to decide if you'll land that big client or get that critical bank loan. Researchers in the Office of Advocacy for the U.S. SBA found that while gender did not have an effect on the performance of a new venture when they controlled for preferences, motivations, and expectations, women had less business experience prior to opening the business, had larger average household sizes, and preferred more low risk/ low return businesses than men.[4]

## THEN WHY DO IT?

Many benefits and rewards accrue to the risk-taking woman with the vision to start a successful business. Although making money is clearly an incentive for going into business in the first place, let's set that idea aside for a moment. Once you start to see the idea that you originally brainstormed on a napkin over lunch with a girlfriend become an actual living, breathing business, you'll feel a tremendous sense of accomplishment and satisfaction. You'll realize you've joined the ranks of the few people in this world who decide to bring a dream to life and take on the personal, professional, and financial risks to make it happen. You'll create jobs where they didn't exist before, contribute to the economic growth and vitality of your community, and become a visible role model for the next generation of women entrepreneurs. My entrepreneurial experience helped me grow so much more than I would have if I had settled only for the promotions and rewards of my corporate career.

Now, how about those challenges? As a woman, your life is a balancing act. You're striving to create a successful business; manage a household; be a great wife, mother, girlfriend, and confidant; and still have time to pursue other interests. Where exactly in the business plan should you write, "Get to my yoga class three times a week," or "Take my husband out for a date on Tuesdays"? In the words of that old Enjoli perfume commercial, how do you get in the mood to "never let him forget he's a man" when you're dog tired from "bringing home the bacon" and "frying it up in a pan"? How will you handle the pressures of every bank in town denying your small business loan applications, creditors ringing your phone off the hook, your kid's school play happening on the same night that your biggest client's project is due, or your rock star employee resigning after you closed a major business deal?

## Divas Lesson #1
### Define balance for yourself and prepare for your entrepreneurial journey.

## THE "M" FACTORS AND BALANCE

First things first: Before you embark on this entrepreneurial journey, assess your lifestyle and comprehend protecting what I call your "M" factors:

1. Money

2. Marriage and/or Motherhood

3. Mortgage

4. Mercedes (or whatever is your "Motor Vehicle")

5. (Peace of) Mind

There may be others you will add, but the point is to know what's important in your life so you can prepare yourself for being an entrepreneur. Building a business will test the strength and stability of each of your Ms, requiring you to be absolutely clear about how you're going to balance the demands and rigors of running your business.

The Ms will be exposed to these demands at various points in time as you travel on your journey. When you think about your roles and responsibilities in life in this context, you are forced to carefully determine your priorities, negotiate them with your loved ones, and draw the boundaries that you never want to cross. You must be clear with everyone and with yourself about where you stand.

Business ownership is at once challenging, engaging, stressful, and exhausting on many levels. Think about how you're going to bring your "whole self" to your venture. You are a multi-faceted, multi-talented woman with credentials, expertise, experience, and knowledge. But that's only half of your story. You also must consider how the day-to-day stresses of running your business will affect your overall health and well-being.

DIVAS DOING BUSINESS

## Mental Impact

Entrepreneurs are often described as "ideas people" who are always thinking, contemplating, strategizing, and making decisions about the business all the time. Even in my so-called "down time," I often wake up in the middle of night with all kinds of ideas. You, too, will find yourself brainstorming constantly with yourself, advisors, mentors, friends, and anyone else who'll take the time to listen to you as you figure out how your business can be successful.

## Physical Impact

Long days and nights are the story of entrepreneurs' lives, especially if you're like me and simultaneously working a "day job." This has a significant effect on your ability to eat properly, exercise, relax, and recharge. I often experience days when I realize too late that I have not eaten all day because I was rushing from place to place and task to task.

## Spiritual Impact

Your spirit keeps you "glued together" regardless of your religious beliefs or the values by which you live your life. I have encountered many challenges in business, including contentious legal situations and ethical dilemmas, which could have broken my spirit without that strong spiritual foundation.

## Emotional Impact

In the normal course of everyday business, you must interact with other people to get the job done, even if you're operating solo. Therefore, emotional stress can emerge at any time. Whether it's dealing with employees, business partners, and suppliers or negotiating contracts or legal agreements, there are times when conflicts arise, arguments ensue, or disagreements impede progress toward your goals.

## Financial Impact

For most small businesses, getting access to capital is the biggest obstacle to achieving profitability and long-term success. This obstacle grew even larger in the fall of 2008 when the banks slammed the brakes on lending to businesses and consumers in the wake of the most serious financial crisis facing the world in generations. With the collapse of the housing and financial markets that hurtled the world into a recession, it's going to be tough to make the payroll, meet commitments to your suppliers, pay bank loans, keep credit-card debt manageable, and cut costs without sacrificing service and quality. You'll need to hustle to keep your financial house in order through the downturn.

## YOUR "FIVE"

T-Mobile recently ran a series of TV commercials asking, "Who's in Your Five?," referring to the top-five people on your cell phone's call list. For your business, you absolutely need to identify your "Five," the key members of your support team. These are the people who will advise, consult, and comfort you when you need to reach out. They should be honest, ethical people who bring you positive energy, encouragement, understanding, and support.

In my case, I have a diverse set of mentors and confidants who form my circle of support. These men and women possess a wealth of expertise and knowledge and help me in different ways depending on the situation:

- **"The CEOs"**: A handful of traditional corporate "white guys" who run big public companies or sizeable private firms. I rely on this group for their ability to think big and quickly get right to the heart of any matter. They often give me the hard dose of reality I need to temper my eternal optimism.

- **"Fellow Divas"**: Women entrepreneurs, all from different backgrounds, who have built their businesses into successful enterprises. They serve as my role models and advise me on all aspects of running my company.

- **"The Strategists"**: A man with a corporate gig and side entrepreneurial ventures and investments; one of my former Intel managers who's now an entrepreneur; and a woman who was one of my MBA classmates with a career spanning academia, family-owned businesses, and Corporate America who all have that unique ability to

DIVAS DOING BUSINESS

look at my strategy and help me generate ideas. When I'm backed into a corner and feel like I have no way out, the Strategists present multiple pathways to a resolution.

- **"The Cheerleaders"**: My friends and family who answer those late-night phone calls when I'm in tears and think I cannot go on another day. They are the ones who say, "So what you're in debt up to your eyeballs and cannot pay the landlord this month? Keep your dream alive, girl!"

Our mothers were so right when they warned us that if we surround ourselves with people who don't have anything going for themselves or don't have others' best interests at heart, it won't be long before they're taking us down with them. Most people don't have the courage to take the risks we're taking. They are busy collecting paychecks at jobs they complain about and don't enjoy, making it far too easy for these naysayers to advocate their "doomsday" point of view. This may sound a little "Oprah-esque," but if you believe that starting your own business is the right course for you to take and you can visualize yourself at the end of the journey having achieved your goal, then you WILL do it.

And now I *will* quote Oprah: "Every one of us gets through the tough times because somebody is there, standing in the gap to close it for us."[5] You need to find people who support you in your endeavors and want to see you make your dreams come true.

# PREPARING FOR THE JOURNEY:

## PEGINE ECHEVARRIA
### Professional Success Coach, Motivational Speaker, and Author

Pegine Echevarria gives a whole new meaning to the term "Bronx Bomber." This native New Yorker and feisty Latina of Puerto Rican heritage has truly "been there, done that" and has the battle scars to prove it. Raised by a determined single mother who struggled to keep her daughters on the "straight and narrow," Pegine used her trademark sharp wit and dynamic personality to work her way from being a former girl gang member to becoming one of the most dynamic, in-demand professional coaches and motivational speakers.

With a client list that includes Bank of America, Verizon, Merrill Lynch, Lucent Technologies, NASA, and the U.S. Department of Defense, Pegine uses the power of her natural comedic gift and magnetic personality to inspire others to greatness. As a young woman, she waited tables and saved her money to move to Europe to turn her life around, launching two businesses, both of which she sold at a profit. She returned to the U.S. to finish her degree in improvisational and audience-participation theater and earn a masters degree in social work, concentrating on group and organizational development.

Along the way, she designed and directed a Latino family support center that *The Harvard Group Review* named as one of the top ten in the country. She launched a thriving professional speaking business that touched thousands of lives and empowered people to be leaders in their work, families, and communities. She even worked as a stand-up comedian, honing her craft on the comedy-club circuit for a couple of years. Her bold humor, enthusiasm, and messages of empowerment have endeared her to audiences, moving Mark Victor Hansen, co-author of the *Chicken Soup for the Soul* series, to describe her as "The WOW of Wows!"

Pegine's success has led to frequent appearances on national talk shows, including "The Montel Williams Show" and "The Queen Latifah Show," and to be a sought-after expert for CNN, MSNBC, National Public Radio, *Wall Street Journal, New York Times,* and *Chicago Sun Times.* She has received numerous awards and honors, most recently being the first Latina inducted into the Motivational Speakers Hall of Fame, which includes such luminaries as Dale Carnegie, Zig Ziglar, and Tony Robbins. She also has written several books, including *Sometimes You Need to Kick Your Own Butt*; *For All of Our Daughters*, a guide on how to mentor young women and girls; *White Guys Are Diverse, Too!*; and *Bragging Rights*: *Transform Your Team in 21 Days.*

Pegine is an active leader in non-profit and community organizations, including Employers United for a Stronger America, a foundation that provides research, philanthropy, and education for employers and their U.S. Military Reserve and National Guard employees; the Society for Human Resource Management's National Workplace Diversity Expertise Panel; the Jacksonville, Florida Women's Business Center; and the National Speakers Association. Pegine lives in Florida, and she and her husband have a son Kenneth, a National Guard solider, and a daughter Andrea, a U.S. Army ROTC cadet at MIT & Wellesley.

Pegine Echevarria, nationally known, well-respected leadership empowerment guru. A kind, warm-spirited woman who leads in a diverse world with laughter and gusto. Our advisor on the importance of ensuring you are ready for your entrepreneurial journey.

# Q&A with Pegine

**Q: What is it about "right here, right now" that is fueling the trend of women choosing to go into business for themselves?**

A: From my perspective, three key phenomena are driving more women in the direction of starting their own businesses:

1. They decided to have children, and having earned advanced degrees like MBAs, may have left their corporate jobs and are now looking for ways to be with their kids and create a business to continue to use their minds and make money. By starting a business, women can have financial wealth and stability and can determine the lifestyle they want. Women can certainly earn a lot of money moving up the ranks at a company, but there are no guarantees. As an entrepreneur, you determine your own course and benefit from freedom in that.

2. Over the past 20 years, the "Baby Boom" generation has been building their careers, and as they hit their late 40s and early 50s, they are realizing that they can leave their corporate jobs. They have significant savings in their 401ks and their pensions and their kids are out of the house. They are ready to focus on themselves now.

3. At a particular point, something "gnaws" at women to nurture their own souls because they've done all they can do in the organizations where they've worked. There's something deep within them, a calling to a higher level of contribution and leadership to create more value that they cannot accomplish within the large corporate organizations. This calling is telling them, "I have to do that" and they know within themselves that this is the time because they are so aware of how things can be made better. They get tired of fighting for change at their companies. Once you've worked for enough jerks, you say, "I may as well just work for myself."

**Q: The risks that entrepreneurs take are so much more personal than those taken in the corporate world. Our business decisions have a direct impact on our personal, professional, and financial lives. Failure hits us where it hurts. How do you advise women to deal with risk and overcome their fear of failure?**

A: An entrepreneur never really knows the depth of the risks she is taking. From the start, we focus more on the potential gains and try to minimize the risks. It's not until you've been in business for several years that the risks increase, and when you reach your fifth or sixth year, you realize that you're "unemployable." All the risk that you've taken gives you the strength and sense of belief that you can do it – and keep going – because you've evolved as a person. You've become richer and deeper as an individual. People who give up and walk away risk losing the opportunity to experience the depth and breadth of character gained by the entrepreneurial experience.

**Q: Let's talk about something that's one every woman's mind: How do you balance all of the demands in your life? Most women entrepreneurs are already leading full lives as wives, mothers, professionals, volunteers, activists, friends, and providers in a number of different ways. Can we really don the "Superwoman" cape and do it all? Doesn't something have to give?**

A: Something always gives yet we perpetuate the myth that we can have it all and do it all at the same time. When we try to do too much, something always suffers. Your marriage suffers, your kids suffer, and your business suffers. Women need to make clear choices at different times of our lives.

When my kids were little, I worked full-time, I was writing a book and volunteering at the school, and next thing I know, I contracted a rare stress disorder that landed me in the hospital for a couple of weeks. My whole body shut down, and my doctor was this old guy who said to me quite simply, "Pegine, it's a lot cheaper to go on a cruise." He was right!

I needed to step back and evaluate all of things I was choosing to do. That's when I decided to open my own business and structure it in such a way that it allowed me to be with my family, accomplish my work, and achieve balance. I chose the slow and steady path. I wasn't expecting to be a multimillionaire at the start. Not that I didn't want to, of course, but I needed to go slow and steady. I worked from 9:00 a.m. to 3:00 p.m., and during those hours, I focused on business. After 3:00 p.m., I put on my "mommy hat" and did all of the things that go with being a mom. I knew what it was like to be a child and not have a parent around. Those experiences fed my business and added depth and dimension to my work that I would not otherwise have had.

I worked my business around my kids and created a clear five-year plan that addressed what the business would look like strategically. I figured out who I needed to meet and what kind of publicity I needed to generate. I determined everything I would need to make the business a success once my daughter finished school. When I look back on that time, I might lament that I wasn't as successful at my business, yet my kids have grown up to be great adults.

I met with a mentor and advisor recently who landed a million-dollar deal. He was reflecting on how it took him 20 years to become an overnight sensation. That's a testament to dedication for the long-term, and now I'm looking at my next 20 years and what I want my business to be. I do have it planned in my head but that plan is flexible enough to change because I know I have to be open to change if I'm going to achieve my goals.

**Q: How can women hone their leadership skills to become successful entrepreneurs who maintain excellence, insist on integrity in their operations, and have a balanced life with room for personal growth, creativity, and innovation?**

A: The first thing you can do is to take the time every day before you walk into your business to appreciate what you have and where you've come from and the other people who've helped you along the way. Leaders who don't appreciate their own skills and acknowledge what they have achieved risk forgetting they are leaders. Entrepreneurship can be a lonely business, even if you have a staff around you.

Decide what qualities and values are most important to you and your business. For me, it's providing ultimate customer service. In my company, we bend over backwards to ensure that we deliver to our customers what they want and what they deserve. At the same time, we make sure our fees are covering our costs and allow us to make a profit because perceived value goes down if you give too much away. Finally, it has to be fun. I like the people I work with and the projects I'm doing. A friend of mine with her own business has a sign at her office that says, "We don't work for jerks," and she's very serious about it. She has "fired" customers in the past because their behavior was inconsistent with her values.

---

**Q: I think all business owners go through times when nothing seems to be going right. What strategies can women use when the pressures of the running their business seem too great and they begin to feel as if their lives are falling apart?**

A: I'm a stickler about being aware of my own self-centeredness. It's easy to forget about the people around us who can give us strength and encouragement. Who's in a relationship with you? Who is going to be hugging you? Who's cuddling underneath the blanket with you? You're more powerful when you acknowledge and appreciate the people who are standing by you. Besides, the cuddling underneath the blanket is a great stress reliever and there's nothing wrong with a little "afternoon delight" to make you appreciate being a woman! If we cannot we do that on our own schedule, then why are we in business?

Also, get into a support group. I have a "Goddess Group" of women small business owners that I meet with on a regular basis. Join professional associations. Have people around you who will smack you and say, "Cut the crap. Reality does not revolve around you." I volunteer with cancer patients and their families and nothing gives me a reality check quicker than being exposed to people who have more trials and tribulations than I do.

[ 29 ]

**Q: Running a business requires you to tap into places within yourself and call upon others to help you with reaching your fullest potential in order to succeed. How can you find out what you're capable of accomplishing as an entrepreneur before you're put to the test?**

A: You don't know. When you start your own business, you have to be willing to get comfortable with being uncomfortable. The more uncomfortable you feel, the more gains you'll get. If you're comfortable, you're doing the same thing over and over and that doesn't bring success. The willingness to put yourself into situations where you say, "I cannot believe I'm doing this," will challenge you to reach the next level.

And yes, sometimes you'll feel like a fake or an imposter, but keep plugging along anyway because you'll find that you're actually the real thing! Imagine you're in a boat on the lake and you can't paddle the boat well enough to propel it forward. But you're moving and you look good doing it. Believe that you're going to make it because when you get to the other side of lake, you'll say to yourself, "Girl, look at you out there doing it."

I was working on landing a major company as a client for over a year and not getting anywhere. I saw the CEO speak at an event and got his card after his speech. When I got home, I called him. I said, "What's the worst thing that could happen?" Well, we closed a six-figure contract with him. If you had told me even 30 minutes before I asked for the card that I'd do it, I'd say, "No way!"

After 9/11, my business collapsed. Every single contract got cancelled. There was nothing. I did stand-up comedy, which I still cannot believe I did. The experience made me a 100 times better speaker and consultant because I forced myself to be funny and I was NOT getting booed off the stage!

There are too many factors out of your control to make something hit. You have to trust and believe: "God, I'm asking and I know you're going to give me what I want." Walk away with that feeling and act like it is going to happen.

**Q: You have said, "We are each responsible to change and grow in order to accept the blessings of success and share it with others." What have you learned that can be passed on to other women who are aspiring to be or already are entrepreneurs?**

A: My biggest lesson is that within you are steel, strength, and courage that are unsurpassed. You have the ability to create products, services, and businesses that make a difference. Being an entrepreneur is about your spiritual, emotional, intellectual, and fiscal growth. The experience will make you into a work of art that's molded, cut, bent, and sculpted to radiate depth, beauty, courage, and power that you'd never find any place else.

The ultimate gift is that you become the woman that you dreamed of being. I wouldn't trade it for anything in the world because of who I've become. It's so amazingly cool!

*Learn more about Pegine and her company at http://www.pegine.com.*

Now, Divas, you are ready to do business.

# BRINGING THE DREAM TO LIFE

## EVERY IDEA BEGINS WITH INSPIRATION.

## INSPIRED BY A BLACK GRANDMOTHER

Coming from an industrious, hard-working, middle-class black family, I have a strong work ethic. Like a lot of kids who were raised in a single-parent household, I was motivated to start working as soon as possible because I wanted to be able to buy the things I wanted without asking my mother to get them for me – things like a personal telephone line, gas for my third-hand 1977 Ford Granada, Ocean Pacific and Panama Jack t-shirts, Nike sneakers, CDs, books, and magazine subscriptions. (Yes, I was a child of the 70s and 80s!) I figured I could justify any of these purchases with the simple phrase, "It's my money and I spend it as I please." I got my first job at McDonald's when I was 15 and have been earning a steady paycheck and doing what I please with the proceeds ever since.

I inherited this work ethic and desire to not be poor from my grandmother, my role model for the entrepreneur I've become. Working the night shift as a psychiatric nurse in a state hospital in New York City, Grandma also owned a small beauty shop in Harlem. She'd leave the hospital in Queens at about 8:00 in the morning, battle horrendous rush-hour traffic, and arrive at the shop in time to open the doors for her morning appointments. For more than 30 years, Grandma did hair at the shop all day and then went home to her apartment in the Bronx for dinner and a little rest and relaxation before getting ready to go back to the hospital that night.

Growing up, I watched Grandma transform herself from a beauty-shop maven by day to a nurse by night. I spent many hot and humid summer days with her at the beauty shop listening to her banter with clients and make her make weekly appointments like clockwork and hustle for the lowest prices on beauty supplies. Looking back, I realize I had no appreciation for how much effort, energy, sacrifice, and time it took for her to make it all work. On the surface, Grandma was "doing what she pleased" with her money – taking exotic vacations around the world; acquiring expensive jewelry, perfumes, and clothes; purchasing her retirement home in South Carolina; and providing for her kids and grandkids when they were in need. (Hey, my brother and I were the first kids on our block with an Atari video game system and the Trivial Pursuit board game because Grandma bought them for us!) Only when I embarked on my own entrepreneurial journey did I begin to realize that she carried a tremendous load behind the scenes, leaving her little time for hobbies and husbands.

## INSPIRED BY A "KING"

Why do professionals from all walks of life think they can run a restaurant business? In my case, I wanted to start a business that was as far away from my high-tech job as possible. As someone who enjoyed eating out and cooking and entertaining at home, I thought starting a restaurant fit my skills and interests best. At its core, a restaurant has one of the simplest, most basic business models in the world: You buy ingredients and turn them into delectable menu items which people pay you to prepare. You get a liquor license, purchase wine and spirits, and sell them at a great mark-up. You deliver fabulous service in a great location where people seek you out because you have the hippest place in town. We all go out to eat and have a pretty good feel for how it works. Could it really be that hard?

For a few years, I had an idea for a grandiose, all-things-to-all-people, completely insane concept of a combination restaurant, cocktail bar, cigar room, wine cellar, and nightclub in one of the trendiest parts of Portland, Oregon, called the Pearl District. I visualized beautiful, chic people maneuvering through the space, carefully eyeing each other as they enjoyed fabulous food and drinks and took in the modern, upscale atmosphere. I drafted a business plan and sought advice from experts, sharing how I wanted my concept to take shape. At the time, the Internet was fueling the country's economic growth, prospects for my Intel stock options were promising, and I had accumulated a reasonable amount of savings. It was only a matter of waiting for the "right time" to pull the trigger on my options and approach potential investors to raise the $1 million I estimated I needed to bring my concept to market.

September 11, 2001. Need I say more? My plan for this hot Pearl District destination went down in flames with the World Trade Center and the Pentagon and an Oregon economy that characteristically is one of the first to enter a slowdown and one of the last to see the recovery. No way on God's green earth was anyone going to invest $1 million in this overblown concept. My plan went on the backburner indefinitely until December 2003 and the release of *Lord of the Rings: The Return of the King.* The final installment of the blockbuster trilogy hit theaters with lots of buzz, excitement, and great reviews during the holiday movie season. Although we don't generally join the crowds on opening night of highly-anticipated movies, my husband Tom Freeman and I were convinced by a group of friends to make an exception.

All was going extremely well that night. We purchased our tickets in advance and planned to meet our friends at the theater for an early-evening show. Tom and I rushed home to meet each other after work, stopped at a casual dining spot for a quick dinner, and made it to the theater in plenty of time to get good seats, with only about 15 or so people ahead of us.

Much to our surprise, when the theater's doors opened, the customers in front of us rushed in and saved entire rows of seats for people who were not at the theater. They called their friends and families from their cell phones to tell them, "Hey, we got the seats! All you need to do is get your tickets." No matter what row we tried, someone already seated said, "Sorry, these seats are taken." We were furious! Many other customers encountered this same situation, but the theater managers didn't jump on it fast enough,

CHAPTER 2: BRINGING THE DREAM TO LIFE

and by the time the chaos subsided, we wound up with the neck-craning seats at the very front of the theater. Tom and I debated for only a few minutes before deciding not to endure a three-hour-plus movie in those seats. We complained to the manager, who promptly gave us a rain check on the movie for the inconvenience.

Well, that left us unexpectedly with a few hours on our hands. Having already eaten dinner and not wanting to go directly home, we decided dessert and after-dinner drinks were what we needed to wind down from the experience at the movie theater. Since we were out in the suburbs close to our house, we didn't want to venture 20 miles into downtown Portland. As we considered our choices, not a single place came to mind. We wound up at a Starbucks Coffee close to our house, and as I sat there, I recalled my business plan from years before and exclaimed to Tom, "Honey, this is an idea!"

I am convinced that if it were not for that night at the theater, Dessert Noir Café & Bar would not exist today. That weekend, I spun my plan for the over-the-top downtown destination into the smaller, more focused suburban dessert café and bar concept. I researched similar concepts around the country – Finale Dessert Company in Boston, Dessert in Philadelphia, Citizen Cake in San Francisco, Extraordinary Desserts in San Diego, Sugar in Chicago – to refine what I wanted Dessert Noir Café & Bar to be. I visited Boston, Chicago, and San Francisco to see Finale, Sugar, and Citizen Cake firsthand and incorporated many elements from those places into my own concept. I established relationships with a few of these business owners as well as local restaurateurs to learn how to bring my concept to life. I gave my 30-second elevator pitch to friends and family as well as complete strangers to help with honing my ideas. To create my financial projections, I sat in restaurants around town at all times of the day and night tallying diners and hired a college student to go to the parking lots of the shopping centers where I was considering locating the business to count cars to determine how many people to expect at my restaurant each day. Within three months, my business plan was complete and I was ready to start raising funds to make my dream a reality. The world was ready for Dessert Noir Café & Bar, and I was prepared to deliver it. At least that's what I thought.

## Divas Lesson #2
### When seeking inspiration, leave no stone unturned. Inspiration is all around you.

Experts generally advise that your entrepreneurial journeys begin with an evaluation of whether or not you have what it takes to be in business:

- Are you a risk taker?

- Do you work hard?

- Can you endure the trials and tribulations of running your company?

- What skills do you bring to your venture that will make you successful?

The answers to these questions are important, but as women, we cannot ignore our unique ability to listen to our intuition. What inspired you to start your own business in the first place? What did your inner voice say to you when you came up with the idea for your business? Knowing the statistics about small business survival rates, what is the feeling deep down in your soul convincing you that the path you're about to walk down is the right one?

Seek inspiration from many places – spirituality, family, friends, life experiences, entrepreneurs, popular culture, literature, current events, stories of triumph and hope – because when your journey gets tough, that inspiration will keep you focused on the "big picture." Learn to appreciate the significance of the small steps along the way that will bring that picture into focus and provide opportunities for celebration and learning even when the road twists in directions you didn't anticipate. And the road will twist and test you like you won't believe!

# INSPIRATION:

## LISA PRICE
Carol's Daughter

After working all day on the crew of the popular "The Cosby Show" television series, Lisa Price looked forward to spending her evenings and weekends in the kitchen of her Brooklyn, New York, home nurturing her hobby and love of creating fragrances and skin care products. For years, she shared her creations with friends and family. In 1993, she started selling her products at flea markets and craft shows and by appointment at her house. The overwhelming response from customers inspired Lisa to transform her hobby into Carol's Daughter, a unique line of over 300 luxurious, all-natural, high-quality bath and beauty products for face, hair, body, and home, allowing for endless combinations and possibilities for every man, woman, and child, regardless of skin type, tone, or need. Who could resist such concoctions as Honey Pudding, Mango Body Butter, and Jamaican Punch?

Lisa started the business as a mail-order operation. In 1999, she opened the first Carol's Daughter retail store in Brooklyn's Fort Greene neighborhood. Soon afterwards, the media discovered Carol's Daughter. Television shows like the "The Today Show," "The View," "The Oprah Winfrey Show" and magazines like *Essence* and *O, The Oprah Magazine* featured the company and its products, and celebrities like Halle Berry, Erykah Badu, Maya Angelou, and Rosie Perez became fans of the brand. Jada Pinkett-Smith even became an investor and she and Mary J. Blige are celebrity spokespeople for the company. In August 2005, Lisa launched Carol's Daughter's flagship store in Harlem, with plans to follow with retail stores around the country.

DIVAS DOING BUSINESS

Lisa, a wife and mother of three, is also the author of *Success Never Smelled So Sweet: How I Followed My Nose and Found My Passion.* Her memoir tells the extraordinary story of how she, as a young black woman, went from bankruptcy to successful entrepreneur, generating more than $2 million a year while she was working in her home by simply following her heart and having faith that she was on the right path to success.

## Q&A with Lisa

**Q: Your mission for Carol's Daughter states that your company is "dedicated to providing exceptional products inspired by nature with a love for family to enhance ones sense of well being." How does nature inspire you?**

A: Nature provides an abundance of colors, textures, and smells that inspire the products I create. When I look at flowers, for example, I immediately think of the fragrances. When I think about the decorations for packaging and gift boxes, I look to elements that are already beautiful by design and stand on their own – sea shells, leaves, fruits, dried flowers – because if you take their natural beauty and incorporate even the slightest minor adjustments, you will create a work of art.

**Q: What was the "Ah-ha!" moment that led you to move from creating beauty and skin care products in your kitchen to establishing your company?**

A: It was August 1993 and I was tinkering in the kitchen. "The Oprah Winfrey Show" came on TV, and the topic that day was women who started their own businesses with little or no money. That got me thinking, "Hey, I could do this!" and I began to take steps toward turning what was my hobby and passion into a real business that would help me make a living.

**Q: Your mother was a strong influence in your life, so much so that you named your company after her. What inspirations did you glean from your mother and you apply to your business?**

A: My mom always had the "glass is half full" outlook on life, despite living her entire life with polymyositis [a rare neuromuscular disease]. Right up until the day she died, she approached life with a "can-do" spirit: "I may be sick, but…"

As I was building my business, my mom always reminded me of the silver lining in the clouds when things got tough. When she died, I learned how to remind myself of the silver lining so I could keep going and keep believing that I was on the right path for success. Despite the challenges I face, the glass is half full.

**Q: We all face hardships in our lives, and when running a business, you're tested time and time again. You even overcame bankruptcy. How did you keep yourself on track in the early days as the business was getting started?**

A: Honestly, I never looked at it as something that was difficult. It was what it was. Because of the financial situation I faced, I knew I had to take things slowly. I couldn't borrow any money; so whatever I invested in the business, I needed to have right then and there to make things happen. I kept my day job while managing the business because I didn't want to sacrifice the income I needed to support my family and make the business successful. Time management was tough because I had long days and nights, but I balanced the load and set my priorities to make sure that I managed it all without comprising any one element in the process.

**Q: Where do you turn for inspiration now that you're growing and taking the business to new heights?**

A: For inspiration, I surround myself with people in whom I can confide and trust, who will listen when I need to be heard, and who let me be myself. My family keeps everything in perspective. With all the opportunities the business brings – the celebrities, publicity, visibility in the community – it's easy to get caught up in that spotlight. When I feel myself getting caught up, I know I can always look to my family and the modest lifestyle we've chosen to live to keep me grounded.

---

## Q: What's next for you and Carol's Daughter as you're writing the next chapter for your company and your life?

A: Right now, I'm striving to keep things in perspective and in balance. Carol's Daughter forces me outside of my comfort zone and challenges me to do new things that I may not want to do or don't think I can do. I'm humbled as I travel on this journey of learning and discovery and I gain more confidence and faith and become more relaxed every day. I'd like to see myself at 80 years old, still stretching myself and doing something new.

*Learn more about Lisa and her company at http://www.carolsdaughter.com.*

# CHAPTER 3

# THE BUSINESS PLAN IS YOUR HOLY BOOK

## WRITE IT YOURSELF.

## "HEY, I'LL WRITE THAT PLAN FOR YOU..."

Your business plan is your "holy book," the single most important document you will create. Many would-be entrepreneurs find it difficult to write a business plan because it is the one place where you must thoroughly explain your idea and the rationale for its success.

- What is your business all about?
- What are your strategies for bringing it to market?
- Who are your competitors?
- How will your product be designed and manufactured?
- Where will you sell it?
- Who is the management team?
- How will you run your operation?
- How will you fund it?
- How will you make money?

When you consider the effort and energy required to pull all of this information together into a clear, cohesive business plan, it's no wonder that only 31 percent of small business owners surveyed in the Wells Fargo/Gallup Small Business Index released in August 2006 wrote a business plan before they started.[6] Yet with over two-thirds of entrepreneurs "planning as they go," an entire industry has emerged to supply aspiring entrepreneurs with business plans. Software programs generate complete plans automatically. Consultants offer writing services, touting their extensive experience and sure-fire methods for attracting capital from investors and banks. Every small business web site seems to have sample plans, templates, and spreadsheets for free or for sale that are designed to save you time. If you're not careful, though, these shortcuts can turn into a long way around.

It's important that you put in the requisite time and effort to write every single word and crunch every single number in your business plan yourself. Writing your plan forces you to do the background research, deep thinking, and investigation needed to delve into every aspect of your business.

Let's say you're opening a women's clothing shop and need information about the economic outlook for the women's retail market in your area. If you purchase cookie-cutter software with a pre-written plan for a women's clothing shop or you use someone else's sample business plan, it's too easy to consider that "good enough" and you could potentially miss local trends in your specific market.

Templates and spreadsheets are tools you should use to get started or generate ideas for your business plan. They are not substitutes for creating the official document. To help you organize your thoughts and point you in the direction of additional resources, I've included a copy of my business plan for Dessert Noir Café & Bar in Appendix A. But remember: This is just another guide to help you create the plan that's right for your unique business.

## OVERCOMING STEREOTYPES

As women, we may be confronted by the pre-conceived notion that we are not business-savvy leaders with ventures worthy of investment. Gini Dietrich, president of Arment Dietrich, a 10-person public relations firm in Chicago, confronts this bias on an ongoing basis: "At least once a week, I'm asked, 'Where's your husband?'" So Dietrich was compelled to create an identity for "Charles Arment" as the "chairman of the board." From her perspective, why fight the battle if the perception is that a man needs to be running the business?[7]

In 2006, Lyda Bigelow and Judi McLean Parks, professors at the Olin School of Business at Washington University in St. Louis, proved that despite the significant gains made by women in business, investors still greatly favor companies with men at the helm over women-owned firms.[8] For their study, Bigelow and McLean Parks created a prospectus for a fictitious company that was planning an initial public offering (IPO). They distributed the document, which included information on the CEO's background and qualifications, to people educated in business finance and asked them if they would consider investing in the company. The twist? Although the study's participants received identical materials, one-half of the bios on the CEO contained the name of a female CEO. The other half contained the name of a male CEO.

Do I even have to tell you the outcome? Bigelow and McLean Parks found that the CEO's gender affected everything from what percentage of the participants' money they would be willing to invest in the company to how much they'd be willing to compensate the CEO. The bias didn't stop at financial decisions, either. Despite evaluating identical resumes, the study's participants judged the female CEO much more strictly, concluding she had significantly less leadership experience, would be less able to manage conflict or handle a crisis, was less competent, and would represent the company less favorably in the public eye. Bigelow and McLean Parks concluded, "What the basic model showed was that the CEO's sex had a direct effect on the attractiveness of the IPO. By making stereotypical assumptions about her capabilities, the IPO became less attractive, which means that female-led firms hoping to go public will have a much harder time finding backers, even though research indicates that the chances for success are just as likely, if not more likely, than a company run by a male."

Considering what you may be up against, it is imperative to bring your "A" game when you pitch your plan to advisors or investors.

Being prepared will raise your credibility and the likelihood that you will be taken seriously. You must be intimately familiar with all aspects of your business plan, an easy goal to achieve because you wrote it! You will withstand any challenges to your assumptions, and you will be able to listen for feedback and criticism with an open mind without getting frustrated and discouraged. Case in point: The story of Jim the Banker.

Jim, a vice president of commercial lending at a small community bank, was my first loan officer, and I knew from the moment we met that he would be difficult to deal with. A chain-smoking white man in his 60s who'd been with this bank for many years, Jim relished the power he had over small business customers to approve or deny their loan applications. Because Jim was in the twilight of his career, he wasn't doing much above and beyond what the bank expected of him. Unbeknownst to Jim, I also was acquainted with a young, sharp black man from Seattle who had recently earned his MBA (from the same program where I got mine...this will be relevant in a minute) and joined the commercial lending team at Jim's bank as the VP in charge of commercial lending.

Jim hated restaurants, having seen many restaurateurs looking for money come and go over the course of his career. He was downright antagonistic about my concept, but nonetheless, because his bank came recommended to me from a prominent business leader in the area and I had stellar credit, he suffered through the process, giving me the list of documentation required for the loan application, assuming there was no way I could have it all.

When I showed up the very next day with all of the required documents, including my business plan and financial projections, Jim was shocked. He read my business plan and asked who helped me write it. When I told him I wrote it myself, he began to test me on the details: "In your industry analysis on Page X, you said...." and "When you describe your target customer in the marketing strategy..." When I passed his tests, he proceeded to the financial projections. When he had an issue that needed clarification, he outright ordered me to have my accountant get him a new set of numbers. I replied, "I'm sorry but my accountant takes direction from me. I created these financial statements and whatever you think you need, I will get it for you within 24 hours. I don't pay my accountant to do things I can do myself." (My accountant thought it was pretty funny that Jim even dared "to go there.")

Eventually, I got approved for the loan, but I complained bitterly to my fellow alumnus, the new group VP, about Jim's lending practices, which I found offensive and discriminatory. Jim eventually left that bank, and I hope I instigated it so he wouldn't antagonize another woman entrepreneur again.

## CLEARLY CONSIDER THE EXIT STRATEGY

Generally, it's counterintuitive to think about the end of your business before you even start, but you will be better off in the long run if you have considered an exit strategy in your business plan. Consider your inspiration and why you wanted to be in business in the first place:

- Do you see yourself managing this business for the next 20 years?

- Are you creating a business that will generate income for you to maintain a certain lifestyle?

- How will your death or disability or that of a loved one or business partner affect your operation?

- Will your business survive if your marriage ends up in divorce?

- Do you plan to build equity in the company to make it attractive to a potential buyer and reward your investors with a certain rate of return?

- Do you plan to take your company public with an IPO?

- Is your business an ideal candidate to start a franchise?

As time goes on, you will gain experience and your exit strategy may have to change to reflect the evolution of your business as well as your own personal needs and desires as an entrepreneur. In my own case with Dessert Noir Café & Bar, I planned to expand the business to one additional location either in the Portland metro area or another growing, attractive market, like Las Vegas, Nevada, or Phoenix, Arizona, upon the success and sustained profitability of the original location in Beaverton. I figured that within five years I'd be well-positioned to take advantage of two possible paths to determine the company's future: 1) Continue to invest in the company and diversify into related businesses, like an upscale nightclub; or 2) Sell the business to a larger company with local, regional, and/or national cafés or a local restaurateur looking for an established turn-key operation. (I probably don't have to tell you that things didn't quite work out as nicely and neatly as I planned, and you will read about the challenges I faced with my exit strategy in Chapter 10.)

## Divas Lesson #3
## Don't let someone else's words speak for you.

As Bigelow and McLean Parks found in their study, the viability and potential success of your business idea will be tested time and again. Other people's biases and stereotypes will color their judgments about you before you even walk through their doors. While we are making tremendous strides and progress every day, women entrepreneurs are still fighting to win the hearts and minds of people, mostly men, who make the decisions that will affect whether or not you get the funding, resources, connections, and intangibles that will put your businesses on the path toward success. That's why it's absolutely critical that you are the one who puts pen to paper to describe your vision. Only you can articulate your logic, passion, commitment, and dedication to your idea. Do the work. Don't take any shortcuts.

# BUSINESS PLAN:

## MARGARET WALLACE
### Rebel Monkey

Margaret Wallace loves to play games and knows you do, too. She also knows instinctively that life in the game universe exists beyond the endless shooting, racing, and sports titles that dominate the industry. Witness the success of the Nintendo Wii game console, and you quickly begin to understand the market potential of casual games.

As co-founder and CEO of Rebel Monkey, a New York-based game development studio focusing on casual games, and Skunk Studios, a leading developer of award-winning casual games based in San Francisco, California, prior to that, Margaret set out to change the nature and tone of gaming by developing simple, fun, and engaging titles for the rest of us. Try games like "Gutterball," a bowling game with alleys set in the Arctic, jungles, and other unusual spaces, and "Tennis Titans," which features colorful cartoon characters who are all competing to be the Court Champion.

With a master of arts degree in communication and cultural studies from the University of Massachusetts Amherst and a bachelor of arts degree in mass communications and communications research from Boston University, Margaret's lifelong intellectual and personal interests have largely dealt with the intersection of popular culture and emerging technologies. A recipient of the Congress-Bundestag Scholarship, she spent a year in Germany studying that country's language and culture. These experiences drew her into the world of games and its potential for reaching large numbers of people worldwide.

Margaret has a long history of developing digital content for the PC and the Internet. She spent several years producing and designing games and interactive content for Shockwave.com, where her signature project was Mattel's "Planet Hot Wheels." Before that, Margaret contributed to various CD-ROM and online content projects for Mindscape Entertainment and PF.Magic, developers of the "Virtual Petz" brands, including "Dogz & Catz." On these projects, Margaret experimented with creating online interfaces that tied into her CD-ROM products and laid the foundation for using the Internet as the primary distribution method for enhancing a game's content and user experience. She became convinced that digital distribution would be the wave of the future.

Margaret was recently named one of the game industry's "100 Most Influential Women" by Next Generation, the gaming news web site. She serves on the steering committee for the International Game Developers Association's Casual Games Special Interest Group and is a member of the International Academy of Digital Arts & Sciences. Margaret is a diva who's got game!

## Q&A with Margaret

### Q: When did you know the time was right for you to leave the corporate world and become an entrepreneur?

A: In 2001, Skunk Studios began as a meeting of like-minded people who imagined a world in which game developers could easily create, publish, and own their intellectual property. The owners of Skunk Studios all came from Shockwave.com and saw the enormous potential the Internet holds for reaching mass numbers of people. With these observations in mind, Skunk Studios set out to distribute games cheaply and efficiently using digital distribution over the Internet. As a co-founder of Skunk Studios, I wanted to take on the traditional game industry by bypassing traditional outlets and channels for game distribution and reaching these new audiences.

In addition to making casual games for mass audiences, Skunk Studios wanted to own what we created. I had spent so much time making games for other people. After all my hard work, I wanted to retain a piece of the action. Often content creators find themselves at the bottom of the food chain because they often engage in work-for-hire projects. While there is nothing wrong with working for hire, content creators generally lose control of their creations and they end up generating value for whoever ends up owning the product. They essentially give up the value (the intellectual property) in their company. With that in mind, Skunk Studios sought to own its creations out of the gate.

I've been a long-time proponent of using the Internet and electronic software distribution to reach vast, untapped gaming audiences, specifically so-called "casual" gamers. Whether via the web, mobile phones, or other gaming platforms, it's thrilling to see the game industry embrace digital distribution and these new game audiences. Since 1999, while working at various companies, I wanted to pursue the idea of selling digital content, but I found little support for this vision. My only choice was to start my own company to focus on the creation and distribution of digital content for these mass audiences at Skunk Studios and later at Rebel Monkey.

---

**Q: What was your process for developing the business plan for your companies? Did you create your plan from scratch or did you use a sample plan for a similar company or concept? Did you seek assistance from other entrepreneurs, agencies (like SCORE, SBA), and advisors (consultants, lawyers, accountants, and/or mentors)?**

A: We used basic templates to create our business plan; even so, we pretty much wrote it from scratch. I did seek advice from mentors in the industry, many of whom were already highly successful entrepreneurs.

**Q: When your business plan was complete and you were ready to start raising capital for Skunk Studios and Rebel Monkey, who did you approach to fund your idea – banks, angel investors, friends, and family? How did you eventually fund your business?**

A: Skunk Studios did not seek venture capital. The company was entirely self-funded from the start. We wanted to retain control over the direction of our company and over our destiny; so we funded the company out-of-pocket and through our various deals that were in the pipeline.

Rebel Monkey was a different story. While we had no problems with raising money for specific projects, we found that in order to achieve our big vision of building a connected community platform for casual gaming, we needed private investment. Redpoint Ventures [a venture capital firm that specializes in high-tech and Internet start-ups] funded us to the tune of $1 million. They were the first investors we spoke to about the company – they found us, actually – and they immediately embraced our vision for online gaming and social networking. Also, we structured our deal so that we could achieve this vision in an unmitigated fashion while retaining ownership of the platform and intellectual property.

**Q: What types of potential investors and backers were most supportive of your idea and which were not?**

A: Back in 2001, we were in the midst of the so-called "dotcom bust." The entire landscape was bleak as far as starting new [high-tech] ventures was concerned. What's more, people with whom we spoke, even experts in the industry, didn't understand the casual games concept and resisted the idea that people would pay for downloadable game content. The [industry's] focus was still largely on male gamers who play console titles and not the kind of games that Skunk Studios wanted to make.

In spite of this resistance, we held onto the dream and persisted. Now Skunk Studios is one of the leading developers of casual games. The casual games market is one of the fastest-growing sectors of the game industry. Ironically, many of those "experts" who dismissed our vision are also in the business of making casual games and distributing content digitally. We were among the pioneers, and I'm doing it all again with Rebel Monkey.

---

## Q: How did your business plans "on paper" differ from what actually happened?

A: No amount of planning can take into account life's everyday surprises. A business plan is, in a sense, a living document. It needs to be constantly reviewed and assessed to respond to movement and changes in the marketplace.

For instance, when we started Skunk Studios, we planned to make games for several game platforms, including the GameBoy Advance. After about six months, we realized we were better off focusing our energy on online and downloadable games. A business plan sets the path for success but an entrepreneur cannot follow the business plan to the exclusion of market realities. As far as following a plan goes, successful entrepreneurs need to know when to respond to change and when to hold steady.

*Learn more about Margaret and her company at http://www.rebelmonkey.com.*

# CHAPTER 4

# THE REAL DEAL ON RAISING MONEY

## NOBODY JUST WRITES CHECKS.

## BANKS WANT THE 3CS – CREDIT, CASH FLOW, AND COLLATERAL

The SBA, local government agencies, non-profit organizations, and banks work very hard to create the perception that they welcome women-owned businesses with open arms and access to funding. Take this quote from Joy Ott, Wells Fargo Bank's regional president for Montana and national spokesperson for the bank's Women's Business Services: "The success of women-owned businesses has been amazing, and we hope our latest lending goal sends a strong message that Wells Fargo is unwavering in its commitment to women business owners."[9] And this from Comerica: "As one of the nation's leading lenders to small businesses, we have a deep understanding of what a business needs to run smoothly, evolve seamlessly, and thrive. And we provide it daily."[10]

Certainly, many entrepreneurs manage to secure bank financing for their businesses, myself included. However, I can tell you from personal experience and my numerous conversations with other experienced entrepreneurs, having alternative sources of income (e.g., a day job, savings, investments) that you bring to the table, an outstanding credit history, and a track record of meeting your financial commitments do not guarantee that a bank will lend you money when you need it most. As Bob Hope famously said, "A bank is a place that will lend you money if you can prove you don't need it."

It makes you wonder, "If they're not funding businesses with these credentials, then who is getting money?" Remember Jim the Banker in Chapter 3? Unfortunately, bankers generally are not paid to have a vision into the future, and that directly conflicts with the concept of entrepreneurship.

You are working the plan for your start-up business despite the net losses each month and doing everything you can to increase revenue and control costs so your business stays on the path toward profitability. You can see breakeven on the horizon. Meanwhile, your loan officer is looking at his or her spreadsheet calculations, which are all about today's "Cs" – credit, cash flow, and collateral. These calculations are designed to fund businesses with the least amount of risk to the bank. It doesn't matter how much of another important "C" – character – you bring to the table. While there are exceptions, in most cases businesses that are profitable right now and have of a track record of at least three years of operation will stand a decent chance of getting a loan.

Even so, depending on your type of business, you could be operating for several years – with multiple profitable locations – and a bank will still walk away from your deal. Those of us with service, retail, and restaurant businesses, which tend to be heavily female and have a reputation for being tough, highly competitive industries with high failure rates, give bankers yet another reason to not lend money to us. The sub-prime mortgage fiasco that started in early 2007 and led to Wall Street's meltdown in 2008 effectively has frozen the credit markets, and now the banks are denying even the most creditworthy entrepreneurs financing.

In this environment, as the recession and mounting job losses force consumers to cut back on spending, small business owners are in a terrible bind – i.e., not generating enough revenue to cover expenses and having no access to working capital to get by in the meantime. On the consumer side, most people are so far "underground" that they're endangering the survival of their local small businesses. On the credit side, lack of access to additional capital means entrepreneurs cannot fund day-to-day operations, pursue expansion plans, or hire new employees. Both have significant ramifications on Main Street: Small businesses are the growth engine for jobs and investment in America, and with no "fuel," the engine doesn't keep running for long.

Even under the best economic circumstances, there's a time and place for seeking capital from banks, and it's not usually for early-stage funding beyond a certain level. Most banks will extend your business modest credit lines and loans depending on your credit history and household income. (Note that I specifically said "household income": From a bank's perspective, *you* are the business. Creditors automatically view you as the personal guarantor of a loan or credit line, regardless of your company's financial position. Until you start generating significant revenue and profits and can separate yourself from the business, it's the cross we all bear.)

What about all those web sites and resource centers that assist women who want to start their own businesses? One thing is certain: The people behind those resources don't write checks. You can get all kinds of help writing your business plan, locating available sources of funding (which usually are banks), success stories, market research, tips, and how-to guides on topics ranging from finding an accountant to hiring your staff. But again, none of these organizations is handing out free money.

What should a woman do to get funding for her business?

## ANGEL INVESTORS CAN BE HARD TO FIND

An angel investor is a person who provides investment capital for the start-up or expansion of a business. Angels are usually looking for a higher rate of return than they would expect from traditional investments and may want to play an active role in the management of the company.

I haven't attracted traditional angel investors for my company because unless you have the next Chipotle restaurant chain on your hands, finding cash-rich investors who are interested in service-oriented, slow-growth, labor-intensive, low-margin businesses like restaurants is extremely difficult. Generally, angel investors want a return on their investment quickly. They're looking for double-digit growth within the first three years. These investors tend to concentrate on technology, biomedicine, and other high-growth industries.

That's not to say I have abandoned the hope that an angel will "descend from the heavens" and bestow upon my business the cash I need for working capital or to lay the foundation for my growth strategy. Angel investors are like the lottery: You keep playing because you might hit the jackpot, but you know deep inside that it's a long shot and the odds are stacked against you.

Still, it doesn't hurt to get out there and try. I'm not afraid of the blind pitch because I never know who might be out there looking for my type of deal. I found one of my mentors, the CEO of a mid-sized public company in Portland, this way. While he didn't invest in my business, he proved to be a valuable advisor, making connections for me and offering me sage advice about running my business.

To find potential angel investors, I hit web sites, newspapers, magazines, personal contacts, networking events, conferences, seminars, trade shows, and every place and method I can think of on a regular basis. Check out my "elevator pitch" that I posted to a web site for angel investors and entrepreneurs and as an entry in my blog: http://moniquehayward.blogspot.com/2008/08/elevator-pitch.html. (To Robert De Niro, I'm still waiting for your response and hope you liked the Valrhona Earl Grey Truffles I sent with my investment proposal.)

While more high-net-worth women have become angel investors in recent years, it is still largely a man's domain. One of my male mentors once warned me to proceed with caution when pitching my business to potential investors because, in his words, many men are only thinking about "one thing" with a woman, regardless of the situation or circumstances. He went on to suggest that the men I'd meet with talk about investing in my business would fall into three categories:

1. They only want to sleep with me and won't invest a dime in the business.

2. They admire and respect me as a businesswoman and will be advisors and mentors who will give me advice and access to their networks, but they won't invest a dime in the business.

3. They will consider investing a dime in the business and expect me to sleep with them in return.

At first, I thought this was completely ridiculous and laughed it off. I thought potential investors, regardless of their gender, would view me with respect and professionalism. As time went on, however, I couldn't believe what was happening to me in many of these meetings – the up-and-down looks, sexual innuendo, and in some rare instances, outright propositions and advances. I've wasted precious time with countless average guys who "kick tires" as if they are going to invest in my business and have absolutely no intention of doing so because they're treating the situation like "The Dating Game." They performed their parts as actors on this stage beautifully by asking for executive summaries and financials to evaluate the business, entertaining me at lunch or dinner meetings, visiting the restaurant on several occasions, getting to know me personally, and increasing my confidence and hopes that we may close a deal. Despite my track record of maintaining my business and having a clear vision for my company's future growth and profitability, they all walked away when they realized that I'm all about business and not their games. In other words, "I'm not sleeping with you, buddy. So unless you're going to write a check right now, don't waste my time." Of course, I say this to myself. In front of them I play the part of the appreciative business owner who's grateful for their time and consideration. Whatever.

I've also entertained creative proposals from "vultures" who prey on small businesses. Their game is to "swoop in" with ridiculously low offers or confusing financing schemes after the entrepreneur has done all the hard work of building and sustaining the business. One such proposal involved bringing on investors in a limited liability corporation (LLC) separate from my sub-chapter S corporation solely for the purpose of allocating all of my corporation's losses at the end of the year to the LLC so these guys could get a huge tax write-off. In addition, the LLC members would lend my corporation money for working capital, which would be paid back at a pre-determined interest rate by a certain date.

Let's think about this: Without spending a dime of their own money, these guys would take the entire tax-write off ahead of me and my investors who had been with the business since the beginning. Then they'd turn around and lend me money that I'd have to pay back, which basically makes the entire scheme a zero-dollar investment deal for them. How did that make any sense for me or my company? (At least they didn't want to sleep with me.)

## LOOK OUT FOR THE "TOO GOOD TO BE TRUE" SCENARIO

In today's Web 2.0 era, web sites, online communities, search engines, directories, blogs, and other forms of online communications are spreading rapidly, making it easier for entrepreneurs to conduct business. However, we run the risk of scammers and hustlers targeting us in this open marketplace for their unethical, immoral, and often illegal dealings. The adage cautioning, "If it's too good to be true, it probably is," still rings true, and now more than ever, you must be vigilant to guard yourself against people who take advantage of business owners who simply want to see their ventures succeed in the marketplace.

With the exception of one person, everyone who has invested in my company knew me prior to my asking him or her for money. So imagine my shock and surprise when out of the clear blue sky a so-called venture capital firm called EuroCapital Group contacted me via email about investing in my business. Immediately skeptical, I responded to inquire about the legitimacy of this firm, for the message had a mass-mailing, form-letter feel that led me to conclude it was a blind pitch that went to thousands of people. When a representative of EuroCapital Group responded to confirm the firm's interest in my business specifically and to invite me to make my pitch to the firm's principals in Atlanta, Georgia, I became interested in learning more about how they found me. The investigative reporter in me went to work.

I recalled joining several online communities for entrepreneurs where members post business plans to attract potential investors, share information and tips about raising capital, and offer advice about managing your business at various stages of its life. EuroCapital Group discovered an early posting of my business plan on one of these sites.

Next, I searched the Internet for any information I could find on EuroCapital Group, and unfortunately, it was not very clear where the truth lay. EuroCapital Group's web site had a lot of information; however, one thing that was suspicious to me was that it did not contain a list of companies in which the firm had invested nor did it list the biographies of the firm's principals. Legitimate VCs go out of their way to put that information on their sites. When I asked my contact about why EuroCapital Group's portfolio companies were omitted from the web site, he informed me that the companies complained about getting too many calls from "tire kickers" who were not serious about the process and wasted their time. While that was a plausible explanation, VCs generally provide references willingly and encourage entrepreneurs to contact those companies when they are seriously considering investing in a company.

Then I hit blogs, online discussions, and consumer watchdog sites, and again, the truth was hard to find. There were just as many people who cited negative experiences as positive ones with this firm. I became concerned about the negative comments, particularly ones that referenced off-shore dealings in the Bahamas, because they all unanimously described EuroCapital Group as a scam. However, well-known, mainstream news sites reported that some of the watchdog sites posting warnings about various companies' products and services were being accused of attempting to extort money from the targeted companies in exchange for withdrawing negative comments and feedback on their sites. The situation was getting ridiculous. Everyone's got a scam!

After consulting with a few people and determining I didn't have anything to lose except a few days of time by making the trip to

Atlanta, I decided to confirm for myself and accept EuroCapital Group's invitation to present my business plan. If this turned out to be a scam, the trip would not be a total waste because I used frequent flyer miles for the plane ticket and points for the hotel, and I could visit my family in South Carolina for the weekend.

Prior to my departure, I had several phone conversations with my contact and informed him of the research I had done. I raised my concerns and made it clear that I was not wasting a trip across the country to meet with people who were not legitimate. In response, he provided a lot of information about the firm's process for evaluating investment opportunities and was open, forthcoming, and gracious. He even explained the connection to the Bahamas and presented a perfectly believable story that described the international nature of their investments. He did not take the defensive stance that I expected. He acknowledged all the negative comments, being careful not to dismiss them outright, explained the issues, and offered the firm's course of action to rectify the situation and to get their side of the story heard. In fact, we talked about how EuroCapital Group and other VCs had to be on the lookout for scams in the other direction – i.e., people looking to rip off investors and banks by saying they're looking for investment in companies that turn out to be fraudulent or don't exist.

Transparency and honesty always win in business deals. In their dealings with me, the representatives of this "firm" sent some signals that were legitimate and above board, but they also sent other signals that left me feeling that something was not quite right. For example, the meeting took place in a lounge area off the lobby of an upscale hotel, which initially struck me as strange because I expected to meet at the firm's office. At the same time, as a woman traveling alone, I did feel more comfortable meeting in a public setting. Also, when I met my contact face-to-face, he was 30 minutes late and had his two young daughters with him, claiming to have had a last-minute daycare issue. I thought to myself, "Hmmm… You're meeting someone for a business meeting about investing in a company and you couldn't find one person in the entire city of Atlanta who could watch your kids?" Was this a scammer's tactic to gain my sympathy and to put me at ease, or did the babysitter really fall through? How could I tell?

I went into that meeting with a well-prepared presentation and my eyes wide open and on the lookout for signs of a scam, like hidden fees, costs, and unreasonable obligations tied to doing the deal. My contact shared nothing of the sort, going out of his way to quell my fears and directly assure me that the firm would not ask for up-front money. Joining my contact was the so-called "principal" of the firm, who asked the right questions and wanted to see the right documents. When we were done with the meeting, he praised my presentation, didn't blink an eye when I asked for $4 million over a three-year time horizon, and enthusiastically expressed his interest in immediately moving forward with the deal.

Upon my return to Portland, I expected my contact and the principal to follow through on the firm's interest and work quickly to negotiate and close our deal. For a couple of days, it felt like we were heading in that direction. There was constant email correspondence to tie up a couple of loose ends from the meeting and requests for me to send additional documentation.

I became convinced that EuroCapital Group was a scam when I sent several email messages to my contact requesting a phone call to discuss next steps, and every time he responded to my emails, he never acknowledged my requests to talk on the phone. Every time I called and left a message, he didn't return my call. I finally sent another email message asserting the urgent need to close our deal before I could make some big decisions regarding my business that required our deal to be sealed. I received no response from EuroCapital Group.

And the icing on the cake? During my investigation, I sent an email to someone who had posted a positive comment to a web site about his potential deal with EuroCapital Group. While he did not respond in time to save me the trip to Atlanta, he informed me that these people proved to be scam artists on his deal, too, and in his words, "It turns out they're quite willing to let you fly across the country for nothing." He explained that once EuroCapital Group convinces an entrepreneur that the deal is legitimate, the firm "requires" him or her to set up a bank account in the Bahamas with $25,000 to $30,000 to cover travel and lodging, legal fees, and other "business expenses" associated with making the investment from the firm's headquarters in Luxembourg. Guess what? The entrepreneur never sees a dollar (or euro as the case may be).

Well, so much for my $4 million! I guess EuroCapital Group recognized that I was savvy and sophisticated and would not fall for their scheme.

## FRIENDS AND FAMILY: YOUR TRUE ANGELS

The more likely scenario you'll encounter when it comes to raising money for your start-up business is to approach your friends and family first. As I mentioned previously, only one person who invested in my business did not know me before I asked him for money, and he contributed a very modest amount. All the remaining investors were either friends or family members who had disposable income and purchased shares in my corporation with the idea that they'd eventually get a return on their investment a few years down the road. More importantly, it wasn't about the money at all. All of these people believed in my ability and potential to succeed, and I backed that up by having a differentiated concept with a well-researched, comprehensive business plan and by bringing the majority of the start-up capital to the table on my own so they had confidence and reassurance that I was serious about the business. I was also extremely selective about the people I approached to support my venture, pitching only those who had entrepreneurial aspirations or ventures of their own or who worked in the business world, could appreciate what I wanted to do, and would not lie awake at night worried to death about the money they invested in my business.

> **Divas Lesson #4**
> **When it comes to money, you will be able to figure it out.**

Unless you're already wealthy, you know someone who's willing to write you checks, or you have that rare business that's profitable from the minute you open, you will find yourself constantly hustling like a mad woman to get money for your business. Every entrepreneur has a nightmare story to tell about cleaning out personal bank accounts or begging and borrowing from friends to make the payroll.

Get your personal financial house in order – clear your debts, pay off your bills, save as much as you can – before you talk to anyone about external sources of funding. According to the Wells Fargo/ Gallup Small Business Index released in August 2006, nearly 75 percent of small businesses were primarily funded by the owner's personal savings.[11] If you have a day job, you should not quit until the business generates enough revenue to cover your salary, bonuses, and healthcare. Although the demands of doing both will make you crazy, when your revenues fall short and you need to cover expenses, your paycheck will help keep things going. Also, when you eventually go to investors, friends, family, and banks and they see you're still working in the "real world," they are much more likely to look at your deal. The credit lines I secured were approved because of my day job.

Inevitably, your business will cost you more money than you anticipate. Construction projects will run late and over budget, taxes will sneak up on you, advertising will be expensive, costs of goods will increase while competitive pressures will keep you from raising prices, power failures and bad weather will shut you down and your insurance company won't cover the losses. Unanticipated maintenance projects and equipment failures never seem to happen at a cash-rich time.

At these times, you will not have help from banks or elusive angel investors. In fact, you'll probably find yourself in what I call "bank jail," where you have been in business long enough to have acquired credit cards, established credit lines, and secured loans with several banks and every single one is at its limit. You have no room to maneuver, and to keep the accounts current, you're "robbing Peter to pay Paul." There is no "Get Out of Jail Free" card in this scenario, for sure.

In this case, you are more than likely going to dig deep into your own pockets and lean on your real "angels" who are watching over you, i.e., your friends and family, to stay in business. If you need $1,000, $5,000, $10,000, or $25,000 tomorrow, who can you call to write that check or wire the money directly into your account? In these situations, you will know exactly who you can count on when you need help. You should always have that "short list" of people you can call in a crunch. Chances are you'll find that other women will rise to the top of your list. As self-empowerment expert and motivational speaker Iyanla Vanzant says, "You never know when an angel is going to come right beside you. If you think back through your life and your deepest, darkest moments, it was another woman; it was an angel, a woman who was there for you."[12] Don't ever be afraid to ask for help. And don't wait until it's too late.

You also may be forced to explore creative financing options to meet your commitments and keep the business running. Where the banks have walked away from entrepreneurs, other grey-market and alternative financiers have stepped in to fill the void. "People-to-people" lending is emerging as a popular option for entrepreneurs to fund their businesses, especially if they're not looking for extremely large sums of money. Prosper Marketplace (http://www.prosper.com) allows you to request money for almost any purpose and invite members of this online community to bid for the privilege of lending it to you. Virgin Money (http://www .virginmoneyus.com), formerly Circle Lending, is another company that facilitates loans between friends and family members. In my case, after a simple application process and routine credit check, I posted my first request on Prosper for a $10,000 loan for working capital, and in less than a day, I received enough bids to fund my loan. Prosper transferred the loan proceeds to my bank account within a few days, and I was able to secure an interest rate and a monthly payment that were comparable to what I was paying on other credit lines.

Less desirable are lenders of last resort, the "hard money" companies who provide businesses with sources of quick cash at high interest rates and use everything from your business' credit card receipts and payments on customers' invoices to your paycheck to determine the amounts for which you can qualify. These companies lay out attractive advantages like quick approvals, funding within a few days, higher tolerance for less-than-perfect credit, and no collateral to secure the debt. Tread carefully here, however. Many of these "banks" have extremely aggressive repayment terms and astronomically high interest rates. I secured this type of financing when my business was in a crunch and signed up for a loan with a 52-week repayment period at 70 percent. That's right: Every single week, this company automatically debited my bank account to get their money, and that hurt like hell. Luckily, I was able to repay the loan before the end of the term without penalty, but it wasn't before I paid over 50 percent in interest.

Finally, learn the art of negotiation with your vendors and creditors. Most people will accept getting paid late over not getting paid at all. Set up payment plans, send regular updates on the status of your business, and let people know what's happening when you encounter a seasonally slow period or you get hit with surprise expenses. You will find that most people, especially if they are small business owners themselves, understand exactly what you're going through.

# RAISING MONEY:

## DENISE BROSSEAU
### Invent Your Future Enterprises

As the co-founder of Invent Your Future Enterprises, a professional development accelerator for corporate managers and entrepreneurs, Denise Brosseau is a tireless advocate for women entrepreneurs who wants nothing more than for her fellow sisters in business to get the experience, skills, and money they need to make their dreams a reality. With roots in marketing, product development, and business development in the technology industry, Denise started Invent Your Future Enterprises as an outgrowth of her earlier work with women entrepreneurs as the co-founder and founding CEO of the Forum for Women Entrepreneurs (FWE, now known as the Forum for Women Entrepreneurs & Executives). Denise led this non-profit organization of powerful female executives from 1993 to 2002 and built it into a $2 million enterprise with chapters in seven cities and over $1 billion in funding flowing to the organization's members, earning her glowing profiles in *Forbes, Business Week, Fast Company, Wired,* and *Inc.* While serving as FWE's CEO, Denise also co-founded Springboard Venture Forums, the influential venture capital conference series for women entrepreneurs, which has led to over $3 billion in funding for women entrepreneurs.

For five years prior to launching Invent Your Future Enterprises, Denise ran a strategic consulting practice providing marketing and business planning services to high-growth start-up businesses, non-profits, and Fortune 500 companies. Her clients included Cisco Systems, Global Business Network, Children Now, and The Stupski Foundation, among others.

With an MBA from Stanford University and a BA from Wellesley College, Denise is a well-known, highly respected entrepreneur

DIVAS DOING BUSINESS

and consultant who was named one of the "Top 25 Women on the Web" in 2000 and received high-profile community service awards from the *San Jose Mercury News* and *San Francisco Business Times*. In 2001, *Fortune Small Business* honored her as one of its "25 Women in Small Business" who helped to define small-business success in the New Economy. Spreading her wealth of knowledge and expertise, Denise supports many charitable causes, including holding the vice chair position of the Housing and Human Concerns Committee in Redwood City, California, and serving on the advisory board of five companies and on the board of two non-profits.

When it comes to raising money for a small business, Denise knows how to get it done.

## Q&A with Denise

**Q: What are the key factors you advise women entrepreneurs to consider when they're seeking capital for their businesses?**

A: Any entrepreneur looking for funding needs to have a clear, crisp business proposition that specifically outlines how she's going to make money for her investors. That is the critical factor in most investors' minds. How are they going to make a good return by investing in you? Your family members may invest in you just to be nice, but everyone else is thinking about how much money they will make by taking a risk on you.

Sometimes entrepreneurs get too focused on describing their new idea in all its finest nuances to an investor and don't remember to articulate the bigger picture. How does this idea fit in the industry/ area that they are serving? What other products or services could evolve from this idea? Who are your competitors and what makes you the better choice? What do the customers want? That last question is perhaps the most critical. It is not as important to have created something "cool" as it is to have found a market niche where your customers are clamoring to spend money on your product or service. You are more likely to get funding if you can show investors that people are beating down your door to get what you're offering.

It is important to remember that you are selling both yourself and your idea. Investors will get excited by your passion, your ability to spin a big vision, and your eagerness to run with this new idea. Sell them on why you are the perfect person to start this company and how you have or will identify others to help you make it a success. They are looking for someone with a solid background in the field or industry of the new business. Most investors tell me that when they invest in a business, they are really investing in a team. That's because the first idea behind any business is not usually the idea that ends up being a success. Having a great team in place allows the necessary iterations to take place to get to the final, successful business idea.

## Q: What challenges do women face when seeking sources of funding for their businesses?

A: There are a few unique funding challenges women may encounter, but there are also some advantages. One advantage is that some banks and other lenders are looking to invest in women-led companies. Unfortunately, women tend to articulate smaller visions of their company's prospects than their male counterparts do. While both men and women may be able to take a company to the same point, a woman is likely to outline only her next three milestones rather than spin the big, exciting, new world view that her male colleagues are articulating. I always encourage women to think and talk big! Getting people excited about the possibilities that lie ahead of you once your company is funded is a better strategy than creating an overly cautious business plan that outlines only the next few sales opportunities.

## Q: How do women entrepreneurs find potential investors for their businesses beyond of their circle of friends and family?

A: Start by looking around you and talking to everyone you know. Talk with other entrepreneurs to learn where they got their funding and ask them for introductions. Look for local organized angel investor groups in your area. Ask bankers, lawyers, and accountants if these groups exist as many of them may be members. I also recommend that you think about everyone with whom you have ever worked. What are their financial circumstances? Could they make an investment or might they be willing to make introductions? People who already know and trust you are the most likely to lead you to the right funding sources.

Sit down and brainstorm, by yourself or with a trusted advisor, all the people you know who might be able to invest and then create a plan to approach them. Who might introduce you? Would they join you at a meeting and "talk you up"? Ask everyone you meet if they know someone who has made an investment and in what types of businesses they invest. Then, go one step further and look for experts in the field where you are starting your new business. Even if you don't know them personally, you can approach them as an advisor to your new company. Once you have established a rapport, ask them if they might be interested in investing or know others who would.

On the practical side, keep a spreadsheet or database with an effective reminder system for follow-up. Practice asking for money with a friend or family member or in front of the mirror until you can easily articulate your pitch and directly ask if someone would be interested in investing. Remember that you are giving them an opportunity to make money along with you. If you realize that you may be doing a potential investor a favor by presenting this business opportunity, you may find it easier to ask them for money. Once you have one or two investors, see if they will then help you get more. New people are more convinced to invest when there is someone they trust also making an investment.

---

**Q: Describe a situation when times were tough financially for your business. Who stayed by your side? Who did you think would be supportive but was not?**

A: I am someone who has jumped on board with several risky new businesses and invested my personal time and money in making them happen. Some have succeeded and some have not. I have forgone income for many months on more than one occasion, and

I've been pleasantly surprised by the number of friends who were willing to bail me out with short-term loans or introduce me to potential investors.

What has always been the hardest is admitting I needed help. Once I got beyond that, I have found that all those sleepless nights were usually unnecessary. If I had asked for help earlier, I would have found it.

---

## Q: In the male-dominated world of banking and finance, how do you overcome the negative perceptions and stereotypes of women-owned businesses when approaching institutions for funding?

A: I have spoken to many women about this issue over the years. I have heard their stories of investors who have told them, "Everyone knows women don't make good CEOs,"or pointedly asked them how soon they plan to have children. On the other hand, I know women who have received funding for their companies when they were six months pregnant or were starting companies in a male-dominated industry like semiconductor equipment.

There are as many strategies for success as there are women seeking funding, but a few themes have emerged. First, if you have the attitude that you will get funding and don't take no for an answer, you will get funded. Your confidence and willingness to address directly the topic of women leading companies will often go far in assuring investors you're worth the risk. You might point out that Avon, Archer Daniels Midland, Xerox, and many other successful businesses are led by women. Second, surrounding yourself with a top-notch team will show people that you mean business. Talented teams get funded because people are willing to bet they will succeed again.

This might sound counterintuitive, but there are women entrepreneurs who believe that their success hinged on the decision to bring a man to their side of the table when they were negotiating funding. One successful female founder told me that ever since she hired a male CEO to take her three-year-old company to the next level, she's been "happy all the way to the bank." Her company succeeded in raising millions in funding in record time and she retained well over 50 percent of the equity in the business. She credits her success not only to the fact that the new CEO was a man, but also that he had strong relationships with the venture capital community. Those connections and relationships are a critical component of raising the bigger dollars. When you select your banker or early investors, consider their connections in these communities and think about how they could help you raise future financing.

---

**Q: When describing the day-to-day reality of running a business, you often hear the phrase, "Entrepreneurs can always use more time and more money." At this point in the life of your business, do you need more money or more time?**

A: I'm a workaholic; so I always want more time. Each day when I sit down at my desk, I feel like I'm in a sprint to get everything done that I have set out to do. I could always use an extra few hours. I have tried a variety of techniques to prioritize and manage my time. Some of them have really helped, but if you are growing a business, more time to get things done is critical.

*Learn more about Denise and her company at*
*http://www.inventyourfuture.com.*

DIVAS DOING BUSINESS

# CHAPTER 5

# HIRING ROCK STARS

## YOUR STAFF IS YOUR FRONT LINE.

## NO ONE CARES AS MUCH ABOUT YOUR BUSINESS AS YOU

When pursuing your dream of owning a business, you realize quickly why 90 percent of the population simply works for someone else. Most people are content to show up at a job, collect a paycheck, and not worry about the behind-the-scenes "black magic" that owners use to keep their businesses running.

Keep this in mind when the time comes for you to hire your own employees. Whether your workforce will be hired on a temporary or on a permanent basis, you will strive to hire the best and brightest people who understand and buy into your vision and are capable of delivering it to your customers. The ones who get it will be great employees and invaluable assets to your company. The ones who don't…Well, that's another story.

Your challenge is to find people who will simply do five things:

1. Show up for work ready to perform the duties for which you're paying them.
2. Have a positive attitude.
3. Treat each other and your customers with courtesy and respect.

4. Check their drama at the door.

5. Not steal from you.

The U.S. Bureau of Labor Statistics reported in its September 2008 Job Openings and Labor Turnover Survey that the turnover rate was 3.0 percent, down slightly compared to the previous year as the tough economy makes it more difficult for workers to quit their jobs and new openings become harder to find. Even so, specific industries may have higher turnover rates, like accommodation and food services and professional and business services with rates at 5.5 and 4.0 percent, respectively.[13] Figure you will work hard to keep the "revolving door" of employees at a minimum by investing time and money on training, providing a safe and comfortable work environment, and recognizing your staff with rewards when they perform well. You will be amazed at how difficult and time-consuming it is to get your employees to do what you've asked and paid them to do.

That's because nobody cares about your business as much as you do. You will drive yourself insane trying to get your employees to recognize that when they forget to turn the lights off at the end of the business day, your electric bill goes up and costs the business more money. Despite ensuring they are briefed about special offers and promotions, your employees will give customers the wrong information or forget to mention the promotion altogether. Your employees will feel entitled to help themselves to your products or give them away to their friends because they consider that a "perk" of the job. You will get late-night phone calls about an employee who has been arrested for driving under the influence and learn he or she is spending the night in jail. And yes, there will be days when the entire operation is a complete disaster because one person decides to pull a "no call, no show" on the one day you're planning a big event that will bring you lots of customers.

## ROCK STARS WANTED: COMPETENT, LOYAL, AND DEDICATED NEED ONLY APPLY

When it came to hiring for the general manager position at Dessert Noir Café & Bar, I struck out twice before actually getting on base with someone who could help me manage my business. I hired my first GM about nine months prior to opening to assist me with developing the operations plan for the restaurant. It turned out that he was a con artist who swindled me out of thousands of dollars and stole company property. I improved only slightly the second time around, hiring a woman with a go-getter attitude, great management credentials (on paper), and good references. Unfortunately, she could not manage the day-to-day operations efficiently and cost-effectively. At the same time, I burned through several chefs who, when all was said and done, left my kitchen in total disarray and our staff unmotivated, confused about the focus of our menu, and nearly ready to walk out on me. It was a miracle that we got food out of the kitchen and served to customers every day. It was an even greater miracle that we got any return business. I seriously considered throwing in the towel and walking away.

In June 2005, a gentleman who was a casualty of a failed start-up restaurant applied for the GM position at Dessert Noir Café & Bar. With more than 15 years of experience with both owner-operated and corporate restaurants, this applicant was a rare combination of a chef and operations manager. Generally in this business, you find one or the other – great chefs with little appreciation for the business aspects of the restaurant or people-oriented, customer-service specialists who can't manage a kitchen.

Interestingly enough, I didn't realize this combination of skills was exactly what I needed, for I was prepared to hire both a manager and chef like I had before. With a 2,000 sq. ft. restaurant that seats only 60 people and a slowly growing customer base, this person recognized immediately that my operation was too small for that much management overhead and convinced me that I was better off with him managing the entire operation to get "two for the price of one." Also, he would have complete control over supplier management, employee relations, and budget management. Without a doubt, it was advantageous to have a single person who was accountable to me for the entire operation.

I knew "Brad" (not his real name) was my guy when he met with me and the outgoing GM before his official start date to review our transition plans. He started the meeting by requesting the business' profit and loss (P&L) statements, a list of employees and background on their performance, and the names of the vendors with whom we did business. Hallelujah! In contrast, for six months, I had pulled my hair out trying to get my outgoing GM and the three-ring circus in the kitchen to pay closer attention to the operation, identify opportunities to slow down our rate of spending, and cut extraneous expenses all together. I had also asked her to reduce the number of vendors we worked with because it seemed like I was writing checks to every person in town who had something to sell to a restaurant. As my mother would say, it was like talking to the wall.

Almost immediately, Brad streamlined the operation by reducing the staff and building a motivated team of cooks, servers, and bartenders; creating a menu that leveraged multiple ingredients to reduce food and beverage costs; and consolidating our vendors from more than 10 down to a handful. He also raised the bar on the presentation, quality, and consistency of our food and service. These changes translated into increased revenue, lower net losses, lower turnover, and critical acclaim and awards.

Still, Brad was not perfect. Even though he initially showed intense loyalty and dedication to Dessert Noir Café & Bar, Brad eventually became a liability. First, issues and crises in his personal life began to have a serious impact on our operation. Despite giving him the flexibility he needed and supporting him through hard times with my own money because I felt it was in the best interest of the business, his personal demands soon overwhelmed his "brain space" and the restaurant suffered from his lack of focus on the tasks that needed to be accomplished to ensure our success, such as driving down costs, increasing revenue, and delivering on our brand promise.

Second, Brad never fully bought in to the Dessert Noir Café & Bar vision that I outlined so eloquently and clearly in my business plan. He literally told customers right in front of my face, "I hate desserts." While he delivered that message in a jokingly, sarcastic manner to get a laugh and make light of it, it was clear that he meant what he said. Every single day he went out of his way to tell me that the name I chose for the business was the primary thing holding us back. Never mind that I was successfully earning publicity and generating excitement and buzz about my business. It was not paying off because my right-hand man was working against me on the front line.

Given his background as a chef and manager at larger restaurants, where the environment has slack built into the system and a higher tolerance for imperfection, Brad managed more by feel than by enacting the strict controls we needed to make our small operation successful. His initial focus and attention to the details gave way to a dangerously informal approach in which Brad carried the operation around in his head. It was difficult for our staff to know exactly what they needed to do if he was not around, and when he was there, he could be volatile and moody as well as arrogant and opinionated – the stereotypical "angry chef" with a big ego. The monthly reports I received on costs, inventory levels, labor, and other aspects of the business in the first few months of him taking over began to arrive with less frequency and eventually stopped coming at all.

Over time, Brad, in an attempt to address some customers' requests for more variety, went overboard and created an extensive menu with a myriad of choices for salads, soups, appetizers, pastas, and entrees and a lengthy Oregon-exclusive wine list which attempted to appeal to every palate. Also, it became clear that he was trying to put his own signature on MY restaurant with this gradual menu expansion by moving the concept toward the higher end with more expensive, costly fine-dining characteristics. However, with 60 seats, a small kitchen, and less-than-stellar foot traffic most days of the week, we carried a lot of inventory, leaving a lot of money tied up on shelves and in refrigerators and not generating any value toward the bottom line.

In addition, Brad's approach to portion control was non-existent. He acted like we were the U.N. World Food Program or some non-profit organization, literally giving food away in portion sizes that could not possibly be consumed in one sitting. Many customers got hip to this, arriving at the restaurant in large groups and immediately requesting that we split their meals, which meant they got a 2-for-1 or even 3-for-1. Our more discerning, discriminating customers were appalled at how much food they got and even complained directly to the staff and Brad himself, begging him not to put so much food on their plates. His arrogance and ego prevented him from listening to any of this feedback, including my complaints about costs being too high. I was going broke purchasing to-go boxes and watching whole plates of excess food get dumped into the garbage. I asked him, "How are we supposed to make money like this?" His response: Most restaurants would kill for his food and beverage costs. Well, most restaurants would *get killed* with the kind of costs I carried.

Over time, the restaurant became devoid of any personality. The vibrant, organized, lively, and energetic environment that I had envisioned did not exist. The staff was clearly on edge. We began to receive more and more complaints about service issues and our brand image suffered. I walked into the kitchen one afternoon and had an "out-of-body-experience" as I witnessed the disarray of the office. Papers and junk were strewn across every surface. I watched the staff go through the motions, performing their tasks with little heart and spirit, complaining constantly about every order, every customer, and every little thing. I thought to myself, "This is not the place I built. Somebody has transported me to another dimension."

I allowed Brad to evolve my concept into something it was never meant to be because I sought the wisdom of – and hired people to work for me – who were so-called "experts" about the restaurant industry. I also received a lot of feedback directly from customers about what they thought Dessert Noir Cafe & Bar should deliver in the marketplace. It wasn't until I looked back on the experience and spent time analyzing and soul-searching that I decided that unless I started listening to the voices in my own head and heart, I was going down.

I had drifted away from what I believed was the right restaurant concept for my customers. I was guilty of:

- Managing the demands of my day job.

- Being on the road too much and not being visible or present enough for my team.

- Putting too much trust and confidence in my employees' ability to deliver my vision without direct feedback and guidance from me.

- Hustling too much to keep the business alive.

- Focusing too much on the big picture without implementing the necessary controls to ensure the day-to-day operations were handled appropriately.

- Not firmly demanding what I wanted.

- Getting personally involved and connected to my executive chef/GM, making it difficult to see it was time to let him go.

Unfortunately, it turned out that Brad was also an incredible liar. Customers later relayed stories to me and my staff that he had positioned himself as an owner in the business with the authority to make decisions about aspects of the operation where he clearly did not. He gave customers free food and drinks and perpetrated other frauds and deceptions while working for me. Beyond disappointed, I was disgusted and hurt that someone in whom I had invested so much trust and responsibility could turn out to be such a big fraud.

I trusted Brad to manage Dessert Noir Café & Bar with the precision, attention to detail, care, and professionalism that I expected because my money and reputation were on the line. But at the end of the day, nobody cares as much about your business as you.

Eventually, Brad's personal circumstances forced him to move out of town and resign as the executive chef/GM, but I'm a firm believer that "things happen for a reason" and "timing is everything." Brad's departure gave me the opportunity to promote the dawning of a new age at Dessert Noir Cafe & Bar. I decided not to replace him because I could not tolerate another angry, arrogant chef.

Instead, I gave members of my team the opportunity to step up, and much to my delight, they embraced the challenge enthusiastically and bought into my mandate to get back to basics and execute the original vision that I laid out for this business. We would provide our customers with delicious desserts, great specialty drinks and cocktails, and tasty small plates and appetizers. Upon seeing that Dessert Noir Café & Bar was "born again," the vast majority of our customers were excited and pleased that we were getting back to our core expertise.

That's not to say everyone was enthusiastic. Some customers complained bitterly that the extensive menu and wine list were gone. Although I was sorry to disappoint them, I knew we could no longer afford to be something we were not. I named the restaurant "Dessert Noir Café & Bar" for a reason, i.e., to deliver something unique and sophisticated in Beaverton, Oregon. For great dessert, cool ambiance, tasty cocktails, and savory small plates, come and see me!

## "DRAMA FOR YOUR MAMA": THE SMALL BUSINESS REALITY SHOW

With celebrity-chef reality television shows like "The Restaurant," the short-lived NBC series that exposed all the craziness behind the scenes at Rocco DiSpirito's New York City restaurant, and "Kitchen Nightmares," Fox's show featuring Gordon Ramsay as a restaurant turnaround artist, I often think that I, too, should hire a camera crew to film the "reality show" unfolding everyday at Dessert Noir Café & Bar. Restaurants kitchens are the stage for every conceivable story line and potential conflict known to man, including romance and sexual innuendo on the job, the daily struggles of people who survive on low wages and can barely make ends meet, the temptation to engage in criminal activity, jealousies among attractive young women competing for tips, bartenders who are closet alcoholics, the insane chef who erupts into a violent rage if a customer modifies an order, customers who walk in knowing that they're going to complain about every aspect of the food and service even when nothing is wrong so they can get a free meal, the ongoing battle between hard-working immigrants who are washing the dishes and cooking the food and the lazy, doing-just-enough-to-get-by people who are serving the customers and making the most money.

While the drama may keep things interesting or exciting, research on the differences between the management styles of men and women entrepreneurs reveals the reasons why it's very easy to get caught up in all that drama. In a report titled *Women Entrepreneurs: Turning Disadvantages into Advantages*, Mai Nguyen of PreFlight Ventures cites studies that explain that unlike our male counterparts, women entrepreneurs tend toward "transformational leadership" styles. We encourage open communication, positive interactions, and trust-based relationships with our employees. We go out of our way to share power and information to create an atmosphere where "great teamwork is the dream work" and employees feel empowered to make decisions.[14]

I am guilty of succumbing to the inherent weaknesses of this approach, which include knowing too much about my employees' personal lives, expressing excessive concern about them, and jumping into "problem-solving mode" when they ask me for help. Add to this my Meyers-Briggs personality profile of "ESFJ" (Extroverted-Sensing-Feeling-Judging), which pegs me as a "warmhearted, conscientious, and cooperative" person who wants "harmony in my environment," works with people to "complete tasks accurately and on time," "notices what others need in their daily lives and tries to provide it," and wants to be "recognized for my contributions," and you can easily see why I experience difficulty fighting my natural tendency to allow employees' issues and challenges to have an impact on me or my business.[15]

Needless to say, I hired smart people who have recognized my vulnerability here and have involved me in situations where I must either choose to not be "Ms. Nice Restaurant Owner" or risk the consequences of ignoring personal problems that directly interfere with the successful day-to-day operation of my business. Case in point: Transportation.

It all started when the "Repo Man" paid a visit to the restaurant one day and repossessed the car of a member of our team we will call "Earl." Earl had fallen behind on his payments and did not make payment arrangements with the creditor so he could keep the car (a common occurrence with employees in Earl's pay scale). Instead, Earl ignored the problem and next thing you know, a tow truck was hauling his car away to an auction lot.

I had no idea that this would turn out to be a watershed event in the history of Dessert Noir Café & Bar, causing logistical nightmares and costing me excess time and expense because Earl suddenly found himself without a car. In the Portland area suburbs, public transportation can be a challenge, and there was no efficient or direct bus route from Earl's apartment to the restaurant nor did the route schedules align with our hours of operation. With public transportation unavailable, I proposed a "kitchen carpool" to help Earl get to work on time. Unfortunately, this didn't work either because our employees didn't always work the same shifts on the same days. Then we tried "car sharing," an idea where Earl borrowed a car that belonged to another employee, call him "John," to get to work on John's days off. Then they carpooled on the days when they both worked the same shifts. Well, that seemed to work until Earl needed the car to go out of town every other weekend to spend time with his family several hours away, leaving John with no way to get to work. Like Earl, John lived in "Timbuktu" and could not get a bus or train to work and there were no other cars available to him or anyone else who can take him to work. Oh, did I mention that both of these employees had suspended driver's licenses because of outstanding tickets and other traffic violations?

So guess who volunteered to provide a "shuttle service" and burned up precious time and gas in her car or made other transportation arrangements to make sure the restaurant opened and someone was in the kitchen to cook? That's right, baby – ME.

I often asked myself, "How many owners are sitting around wondering how their employees are getting work today?" or "If I were a man, would I get this involved in whether or not these people could get to work? Would they even come to me with this issue if I were a man?" Your first reaction likely is to think that most business owners, regardless of gender, would simply fire employees with transportation issues because they would view it as the employees' responsibility to get to work the best way they could if they wanted to keep the job. Believe me, I have received that advice and even thought of it myself first.

If it were only that simple. When your business is small and you're going to great lengths to make sure the doors open every day, one critical person's absence precipitates a crisis. It wasn't that black-and-white when I considered that these employees had been with the restaurant nearly since it opened, had demonstrated tremendous loyalty, and were responsible for delivering the award-winning food that graced our tables each day.

One day, my company will be big enough and make enough money that I can afford to create more distance between my employees and me. Then I'll have the luxury of being able to put my foot down and not get dragged into their drama. Until then, the lesson I'm learning is to be mindful of the lines I need to draw. Over time, I've gotten better at keeping myself out of certain situations and conversations to avoid solving my employees' personal problems.

## Divas Lesson #5
### Find the rock stars who will play your song.

Rock stars are hard to find, but when you've got them, understand what motivates them to "play your song" and be a "member of the band." Is it recognition? Is it money? Is it creative freedom? Is it having special projects above and beyond their normal workload? Is it time off to volunteer or take a class? Is it a path to promotion? Once you know the secrets to their success, communicate your vision to your employees in a way that matters to them and allows them to perform their jobs with enthusiasm and a stake in your success. Finally, recognize your own tendencies to get involved in your staff's drama and determine which situations are best for you to remain a neutral, disinterested observer and which require you to provide guidance or a resolution path for an issue that could have a significant impact on your or your business.

# HIRING ROCK STARS:

## SONDRA BERNSTEIN
### the girl & the fig restaurant

Although she was born in Washington, D.C. and raised in Philadelphia, Pennsylvania, Sondra Bernstein feels right at home in the heart of California's Wine Country. She owns *the girl & the fig restaurant* and *estate restaurant* in Sonoma and *the fig café & wine bar* in Glen Ellen, California, and has capitalized on her creative energy and artistic sensibilities for over 20 years in the hospitality business. Sondra describes her journey to Sonoma County as inevitable, driven by her passion for food and wine.

Sondra earned a bachelor of fine arts degree in photography from the Philadelphia College of Art, worked as a trainer and team leader for the T.G.I. Friday's restaurant chain's national openings, graduated from The Restaurant School with a degree in culinary and restaurant management, and served as the operations manager for several critically-acclaimed, award-winning restaurants in Philadelphia (The Fish Market and Marabella's) and Los Angeles (Alice's Restaurant and Tavern on Main) and as the operations director for Viansa Winery in Sonoma County. Sondra is also the author of *the girl & the fig cookbook* published by Simon & Schuster in April 2004, and started her own gourmet food product line is available nationwide under *the girl & the fig* label. In 2006, Sondra opened *the fig pantry,* a gourmet-to-go deli, wine, and gift store, and Les Petites Maisons, four vacation cottages located one mile from the Sonoma Plaza.

For Sondra, owing restaurants in Sonoma County is a way for her to pay tribute to the local farmers, ranchers, cheese makers, grape growers, and vintners who complement one another in that bountiful landscape. She describes her restaurants as "mixed-media collages" that incorporate the five senses:

- Sight encompasses her restaurants' physical space as well as the chef's finished plate.

- Smell, obvious as it may be, is necessary to enhance the diners' other senses.

- Sound would inevitably be the restaurateur's choice of music.

- Touch would show itself on two levels: 1) the textures of the food and the wine and 2) the emotional connection of memories and feelings that the dining experience can bring.

- Taste keeps diners coming back for more.

Below the surface, subtle nuances and details round out *the girl & the fig* dining experience. Sondra has instilled her philosophy of using local products when available, focusing on wine education with her guests and staff through variety and tasting and allowing the staff to contribute in the areas that inspire them. With these values as her guide, Sondra has created a family of restaurants that she believes in, enjoys working in, and fulfills her desire to bring people happiness through a delicious dining experience.

Putting all of these elements into practice requires hard work and dedication, and Sondra has surrounded herself with talented and passionate people who view life as a work in progress. Borrowing from the theater, Sondra believes that you need to start with the real thing (in theater = raw talent, in dining = raw product). From there, it takes refinement and practice to perfect the show before the curtain goes up. Passion, intensity, teamwork, and integrity are the ingredients driving her staff's hard work to a climax, resulting in guest satisfaction and a sense of personal accomplishment.

# Q&A with Sondra

**Q: As a former staff trainer for T.G.I. Friday's, you have a lot of experience managing employees. How do you attract the best talent to work for your business?**

A: Hiring the right staff is critical to the success of *the girl & the fig*. I truly value my staff and I let them know this often. Most of our staff members come to us by word of mouth or are recommended to us by other employees. We try to keep our employees motivated, excited, and happy by asking for their input and using their ideas when it makes sense for our business. We train and promote from within. Many of our kitchen cooks started as dishwashers. If an employee shows an interest and is willing, we will take the time to train him or her in a new area.

**Q: When you interview prospective employees, what are you looking for?**

A: I look for bright, enthusiastic personalities for our front-of-the-house staff. Friendly faces, big smiles, and a caring attitude go a long way in the restaurant business. We don't hire based on experience alone. Sometimes the desire to learn and a high level of enthusiasm will win me over and I will want to work with a blank canvas. For my back-of-the-house staff, personality is always a plus, but I am generally looking for staff members who are willing to work hard and safely and understand the importance of a team environment.

**Q: The restaurant workforce is unpredictable; it's not unusual to have high turnover in an operation, large or small. What are your strategies for retaining your employees?**

A: The cost of training new employees is expensive and time consuming, and the labor market in Sonoma is tight. Because of this, we try to make the best decisions possible in the hiring process. At least two managers/chefs must agree to hire a prospective employee. We give prospective servers a pre-hire culinary/service quiz and have our prospective culinary staff do a try-out or a stage to evaluate their skills and interaction with our current staff. We also get references for each and every employee.

It is important that prospective employees interview us as much as we interview them. We are looking to create long-term relationships. We need to make sure our new hires are compatible with our philosophy and our existing staff.

Our training programs for hourly staff last three to five shifts depending on the department. There is a lot of interactive training, conversation, product tasting, and testing. Our training sets the tone for our expectations. When we hire properly, we have a better chance of keeping great staff members.

Once an individual is hired, we have a 60-day review period and then a more formal review at 90 days. We keep our staff aware of their performance at all times. Open communication, clear expectations, and positive reinforcement are tools that we use daily.

## Q: What rewards and incentive programs have you implemented that work best for your business?

A: We have developed a management bonus program that specifically ties into our managers' performance in the food, wine, and labor areas of our business. This has proved motivating to them and worthwhile to our bottom line. Though we don't have specific incentive programs for our hourly staff, we sometimes have contests and we have yearly MVP awards. We take our staff to wineries for tastings, and though these outings are educational, they view these events as perk. Our holiday parties are also a great reward.

## Q: How do you ensure your employees continue to buy into your vision for the business?

A: Their understanding of our mission statement is an important part of the training. Conversations during training focus on explaining my passion and the deep-rooted concepts of our company's philosophy. Keeping the company's vision on track is a huge responsibility. As we hire new employees, it is important that they understand our concepts and appropriately convey our ideas to our guests. Our employees are a HUGE part of our overall vision and we make sure that they know it!

## Q: Under what circumstances have you had to terminate employees?

A: It takes a lot to get terminated at *the girl & the fig*. Generally, our restaurant culture is such that people terminate themselves if they don't fit in. Because of the time and effort it takes to train our employees, we like to see as little turnover as possible. I also tend to get emotionally involved with our staff and their families. We try to do whatever it takes to help our staff along with retraining, guidance, and counseling before cutting any ties. However, I have a zero-tolerance policy for stealing, drugs, or alcohol abuse and I will absolutely let someone go for doing these things.

## Q: Who is the "rock star" on your staff and what makes him or her special?

A: Our director of operations/executive chef, John Toulze. John has worked with me since the inception of the restaurant. We have grown together, working towards the same goals. His commitment, dedication, and loyalty make him THE ROCK STAR of the company! I have watched him evolve from trainee to trainer, from line cook to chef, from the server to director. He understands the focus of the company and distributes it daily. His efforts have earned him a partnership in the company.

*Learn more about Sondra and her company at*
*http://www.thegirlandthefig.com.*

**CHAPTER 6**

# MARKETING THE BUSINESS

## BECOME A FEARLESS PROMOTER.

## I BUILT IT SO THEY WOULD COME

Entrepreneurs are often guilty of being overly optimistic about how quickly their concepts will resonate with customers and become established in the market. Despite conventional wisdom pointing toward the long gestation period required for restaurants to become money makers, I thought my experience would be different. After all, my restaurant idea was unique and I'm an expert marketer, who with the right story and key lineup of benefits, could convince a man standing in the pouring rain that he didn't need an umbrella. Surely the residents of Beaverton would discover Dessert Noir Café & Bar, a line would form out the door daily, and we'd break even within a few months of opening. Oh, how naïve I was!

Classic marketing textbooks teach you about the "Four Ps of Marketing": Place, Product, Price, and Promotion. Using the Four Ps, I developed my marketing strategy for as follows:

**Place:** I leased a prime corner storefront in a newly revitalized 450,000 square-foot shopping center in the center of Beaverton, Oregon, located seven miles west of Portland and home to 80,000 residents with a median income of nearly $50,000. The space is surrounded by big-name national and local retailers like Office Depot, Borders Books & Music, Best Buy, LA Fitness, New Seasons

Market, Powell's Books, and Century Theatres. In fact, my space is directly across from Century Theatres, making it ideal to take advantage of theater traffic.

**Product:** At Dessert Noir Café & Bar, dessert is the "hero" supported by "faithful sidekicks." While our desserts are the hook, we give folks real food that is just as good. Our menu items are expertly handcrafted and presented, but approachable and familiar at the same time. We wanted our patrons to feel comfortable, not intimidated. How many times have you been in a fancy restaurant and ordered food so intricately and delicately plated that you were afraid to stick your fork in it?

Restaurants shouldn't stop at fantastic food. As Sondra Bernstein showed us, it's also about the experience, and Dessert Noir Café & Bar offers great atmosphere, ambiance, and service just like you'd find in a chic place downtown. The difference is there's no commute. We're located in a spot that's close to where people live and work. We further differentiate the concept with live music, weekly specials, and fun events.

**Price:** Having carved out a niche between casual-dining chain restaurants and fine dining, we focused on delivering the value that customers appreciate in a chain while gently pushing them toward a more upscale experience with our high-quality food and drink and fine-dining sensibilities.

**Promotion:** I'm a marketing and publicity "machine" with extensive experience launching promotional and press campaigns prior to opening Dessert Noir Café & Bar. For example, while the restaurant was under construction, I partnered with a long-established neighborhood restaurant to feature our desserts on its menu to generate buzz about my new place and to get real customer feedback. Then I met with a reporter for *The Oregonian,* our major daily newspaper, who wrote a profile about me and my restaurant which ran a couple of weeks prior to our opening.

Once we opened, I kicked things into high gear by running advertising, direct marketing campaigns, and special events to create awareness and build our customer base. At the same time,

I've secured steady press coverage. Most businesses would kill for the publicity I get: In the restaurant's first four years, I placed over 35 stories in local and national TV, radio, newspapers, and magazines. We've earned positive reviews and local awards, including Portland Citysearch's "Best of Dessert 2005," which we received four months after we opened, and *The Oregonian*'s "Best Bites 2006," which is an annual roundup of Portland's great food finds. I continue to pitch several media outlets and talk shows to build my presence on the national stage. In fact, Michael Turback, a nationally-recognized food writer, included a feature on our chocolate-espresso "liquid dessert" martini in his recent book about coffee and chocolate titled *Mocha.*

With all this publicity, you might assume that there is a line out the door at Dessert Noir Café & Bar." Not quite.

## DECIDING ON A NAME, BEING A PIONEER AT A LOCATION, AND WORD OF MOUTH

My marketing approach to creating a presence for Dessert Noir Café & Bar started with the restaurant's name itself. It came to me as I imagined the space and visualized what people would do there. Inspired by the ultra lounges, restaurants, and nightclubs I had patronized in major European and American cities – from Paris, London, and Rome to New York, Chicago, Miami, Las Vegas, San Francisco, and Los Angeles – I originally conceived a classy evening destination for 20-, 30-, and 40-something men and women looking for fabulous desserts, small savory plates, specialty cocktails, and wine. Although I'm not a Francophile in particular, I decided that the French language would give the place an element of sophistication. I highlighted "dessert" as the primary element, used the word "noir" (which means "black" in French) to connote the after-hours theme, and tied everything together with "café" and "bar" so people would understand that we offered more than just dessert. I envisioned Dessert Noir Café & Bar to be unlike anything that anyone had ever seen in a suburban context.

As is often the case, what made perfect sense to me as an entrepreneur was completely lost on my customers. My name choice meant that I've had to spend a lot of my marketing resources simply educating customers about the concept. No matter how hard I've tried to communicate that Dessert Noir Café & Bar is about more than dessert, we still get customers who think that's all we do, which means there are potential customers out there who have never considered visiting our restaurant due to this misperception. "Café & Bar" seems to get lost completely despite examples in the marketplace of businesses, especially restaurants, whose names focus on a single element but everyone in the world knows they do more than that one thing. Cheesecake Factory's menu extends well beyond cheesecake, California Pizza Kitchen makes more than pizza, and Burger King sells more than hamburgers, to name a few. Even my most sophisticated, well-traveled, erudite customers don't get it – and if they don't get it, then you know the masses don't.

Friends, employees, business advisors, customers, and complete strangers have advised me to change the name of the restaurant, as if taking that action would suddenly put more butts in my dining room's chairs. While I know these folks have good intentions, I also realize it's easy to make suggestions when it's not your money we're talking about. From a marketing perspective, I've spent oodles of cash building equity in and creating differentiation for the Dessert Noir Café & Bar brand. Through press coverage, advertising, promotions, web sites, collateral, blogs, social networking, menus, and other vehicles, Dessert Noir Café & Bar is becoming more recognized each day, making it too expensive to start over. The neon sign on the front of the building alone is a $5,000 investment.

Another uphill battle I'm fighting is my location. On paper, the location is exquisite: a multi-million-dollar redevelopment and expansion of a shopping center with brand-name national and local retailers, a 16-screen multiplex theater next door, and strong demographics within a five-mile radius. The space I have adjacent to the theater is part of the expansion and it did not exist in the original development. Unlike the redevelopment on the main boulevard, where big brand names have staked out their territory, the expansion completes the back side of the center and faces a new road that had to be built to create access to this new area. As the first tenants of the expansion, Century Theatres and Dessert Noir Café & Bar are the "pioneers" for this part of the center. Many shoppers visiting the very visible front side of the shopping center have no idea the rear expansion exists. While this has improved over time as more shoppers become aware of the new developments at the shopping center, we still get the occasional guests who come to Dessert Noir Café & Bar and say, "Wow! I had no idea this was back here."

It took nearly two years for additional tenants to move in and drive foot traffic to our side of the development. When you're a pioneer, it takes a considerable amount of money to generate awareness, and I struggle daily to find innovative, cost-effective ways of driving traffic to my business.

On the other hand, my strategy to "depend on Hollywood" and partner with nearby Century Theatres has forced me to think of creative ways to sustain my business when the studios deliver less-than-stellar movies. In the last four years, with few exceptions, Hollywood has largely failed to hit the jackpot with the type of major, must-see films that typically drive people into movie theaters. If you can recall five movies you've wanted to see before they hit DVD during this time period, I would be amazed. Does *Star Wars Episode III: Return of the Sith* come to mind? No? How about *Mr. and Mrs. Smith*, starring Angelina Jolie and Brad Pitt, two of Hollywood's biggest stars? OK, maybe not. What about *Harry Potter and the Goblet of Fire*? Or I bet you went to *The Da Vinci Code* because you read the book and thought Tom Hanks would knock your socks off. Still nothing? How about *Pirates of the Caribbean: Dead Man's Chest*, or *The Departed* or *Casino Royale*? Maybe it took witnessing Heath Ledger's penultimate performance in the Batman sequel *The Dark Knight* or seeing the reunion of the cast in the movie version of the hit HBO series *Sex and the City*.

These days, suburban families tend to cocoon within their cozy houses equipped with fancy home theater systems and their Netflix subscriptions. Hollywood needs sure-fire winners at the box office to get people out of the house and committed to a night out at the movies. When people aren't going out to the movies, they're generally not coming to my restaurant in large numbers.

Upon surveying my customers several months after opening, I learned that word of mouth from friends and family is by far the top deciding factor that ultimately brings patrons into a restaurant. While press articles, advertising, and direct mail are the tools I use for "air cover," word of mouth is my "ground war." All business boils down to positive (or negative) referrals. When a person speaks highly of you and your business, especially if he or she is viewed as a trusted and credible source of information, the "chain reaction" of spreading the word creates buzz and excitement that money simply cannot buy.

I've successfully generated positive word of mouth about my concept through a combination of letting the word spread on its own and intervening to create the buzz through targeted promotions, sponsorships, street marketing teams, charitable giving, and celebrity appearances. When Oscar-winning actor Morgan Freeman made an impromptu appearance at Dessert Noir Café & Bar in August 2006, nothing got my customers dialing their friends on their cell phones faster than when they walked into the restaurant and saw an A-list celebrity enjoying a New York strip steak.

A common misperception about word of mouth is how quickly it spreads. In reality, when someone tells another person about a business, that does not instantly bring that business a new customer. Word of mouth can be painfully slow, taking months and even years to build in the marketplace. Word of mouth that we generated several months ago is just now starting to translate into actual business.

Think about your own consumer behavior. A friend who keeps up with the latest and greatest places to dine casually mentions a new restaurant during a phone conversation. You make a mental note of the place, but a few days later, you can't remember the restaurant's name and don't bother to call your friend to ask her again because it isn't all that important. A month or so later, you see a restaurant review in the newspaper and suddenly recall that it's the same place your friend mentioned a while back. You clip the article and set it aside. Another month passes and you're having a conversation with another friend who mentions the same place, and you remember that review. Weeks later, when everyone's schedules line up and you and your girlfriends can get together for drinks and appetizers after work, you finally make it to the restaurant. Sound familiar? I'm sure it does.

## WEATHER AND WEIRDNESS: THE FACTORS BEYOND YOUR CONTROL

When it comes to marketing your business, sometimes it's impossible to pinpoint actions you have made that are fundamentally wrong. When you wrote your business plan and forecasted your market and growth potential, you thoroughly researched the opportunities, assessed the competitive landscape, and analyzed the data. On paper, everything aligned. Now it's just a matter of execution. As you go along, you can correct your course to learn from mistakes you might make or capitalize on any successes you may achieve through a particular event or marketing campaign.

On the other hand, there will be times when the only explanations for your ineffective marketing efforts are "weather and weirdness." Taking weather first, Oregon is famous for its rainy season, which usually lasts from about the middle of October until the end of June. Oregonians are accustomed to this pattern and generally don't let the rain keep them from going about their normal routines. But if the sun "peeks out" and we get a break from the rain during this time, I'm guaranteed to be sitting in my restaurant by myself while everyone else rushes outside as if they're never, ever going to see the sun again. With my restaurant being next to a movie theater, imagine my shock in February 2005 when we got a couple of weeks of unusually sunny, warm weather during Academy Award season and no one was at the movies. You could count the number of cars in the parking lot on both hands.

Then there are days when you have no earthly idea what keeps people from patronizing your business. On a Thursday night in mid-October 2006, we didn't have a single customer come in for dinner, and Thursday is usually one of our busiest nights. Did everyone get the same memo simultaneously that said, "Go straight home after work and don't stop at a restaurant" or "Today is not a good day to buy X product or Y service"? Bizarre...

External factors and events also have a way of throwing the best get-out-the-word strategies off kilter. Take sports, for example. Unless you have a sports bar, Super Bowl Sunday will be a slow day for your restaurant, especially if your local team is in the game. The Super Bowl has achieved almost holiday status with people gathering around their TVs to watch the match. That happened to my business when the Seattle Seahawks played against the Pittsburgh Steelers in Super Bowl XL in February 2006. Ever since then, I've closed the restaurant for the "Super Bowl Sunday Holiday." A year later, the University of Oregon's men's basketball team charged through March Madness, making it all the way to the "Elite Eight." Again, my dining room was empty on the Friday night that third-seeded U of O claimed victory over seventh-seeded University of Nevada Las Vegas in a thrilling, nail-biting close game.

Economic factors like spikes in energy prices, the meltdown of the financial sector, the housing market debacle, layoff announcements from major employers in your area, general consumer sentiment, and political issues like the on-going war and conflicts in Iraq and Afghanistan can have a serious impact on the outlook for your business. Factors like these will challenge you to rise above the din of bad news and positively promote your business to give your customers a reason to spend their money with you right now.

## Divas Lesson #6
## Be fearless when it comes to promoting your business.

Don't you wish it were as simple as walking outside your place of business with a megaphone and blasting your marketing messages to the world? When it comes to marketing your business, you have to be a shameless, fearless self-promoter in order to point the spotlight in your direction, attract people to your concept, and convince them to spend their money with you once they walk through the door. To get your juices flowing about marketing for your business, I've included a marketing plan template in Appendix B.

When developing your marketing strategy, you must have a clear, coherent story that differentiates your business from your competitors.

- What is your unique selling point?
- What's the hook?
- What makes your business special and why?
- What is it about you as a person that is unique and interesting and will make the story about your business rich and colorful?

Once you've developed your story, you need to create channels to get your message out. As women, we have an advantage in the business world in that we naturally develop and nurture relationships. Establish contact with a few local reporters who cover small businesses in your community. Arrange a meeting with them so you can learn more about the types of stories they cover and find out the best ways to keep them informed about news and events about your business.

For small businesses, marketing campaigns can quickly get expensive. You can scale your marketing plan to fit your budget depending on how much "air cover" you need versus how much "ground war" you're planning to fight. When you don't have a big budget for print or broadcast advertising or direct marketing, focus on inexpensive tactics to spread the word. Create an informative web site, use email newsletters from sites like Constant Contact, start a blog, and encourage customers to link with you on social networking sites like MySpace, Facebook, and LinkedIn. Distribute and post flyers, obtain press coverage, get your friends to book business with you, give your employees discounts to bring in their friends and family, and sign up for free online and print directories. Do whatever it takes to generate the buzz. Some of these tactics might not work as well as others, yet all you'll spend is a little time and minimal money as you experiment.

Another option that will allow you to get more bang for your limited marketing bucks is joint marketing and selling with suppliers, customers, or complementary businesses. You don't have to look far to create joint marketing opportunities, nor do you have to spend a lot of money to achieve good results. For example, Indio Spirits is a distiller of vodka, gin, and whiskey in Portland, specializing in small handcrafted batches infused with unique flavors. At Dessert Noir Café & Bar, we feature Indio's vodkas in a few of our specialty cocktails. When Indio announced the introduction of two new flavors, Wasabi and Blood Orange, I collaborated with Indio's owner, John Ufford, to host an exclusive launch party at the restaurant where we both invited our customers and the press to sample the vodkas in new cocktails and savory dishes for a special dinner.

Lastly, don't ever stop talking about your business. Everyone you know and every new person you meet represents a one-on-one marketing opportunity. I've been known to hustle people in parking lots to get them to come to my restaurant. When you share your passion, energy, and drive about your business often enough, it will come naturally from your heart and out of your mouth. That's an amazing feeling!

# MARKETING:

## SHERIL COHEN KUNZ
### Girl on the Go!

When she founded Girl on the Go! in late 2003, Sheril Cohen Kunz proved that necessity is the mother invention for real. After surviving a 14-month fight with advanced-stage cancer in her lymph nodes, which included a bone marrow transplant, Sheril was a woman changed but not interrupted. A star marketer on Wall Street, Sheril knew that simply returning to her job as vice president of brand and relationship management at JP Morgan Chase was not going to fulfill and satisfy her in the ways that it had before her illness. Reflecting on her own personal experience as a cancer patient who had lost her hair during treatment and relying on her proven skills and expertise as a marketing professional, Sheril identified a unique market niche to greatly improve the wig-shopping experience for cancer patients, a process that she describes as making you feel as exposed as "trying on a bathing suit in a public parking lot." To help women through this difficult period in their lives, Sheril decided it was time to offer a high-quality in-home wig shopping experience with privacy, compassion, and convenience built in. Ladies, no more ducking and dodging from one wig shop to the next to maintain your privacy and no more ill-informed, unmotivated salespeople who want to sell you tacky wigs that don't remotely resemble your style and personality.

Girl on the Go!'s roots are in New York, but the company's wig consultants also operate in New Jersey, Connecticut, California, Massachusetts, North Carolina, Pennsylvania, and Wisconsin. Think of them as the "Mary Kay Lady" for wigs, caring professionals who come to your home and offer practical advice on wig fit, style, and care. With demand for her services increasing beyond her current territories, Sheril added an online service called "Look Just Like You." Customers submit a photo of themselves with the hairstyles they want to re-create, include a swatch of their hair, and their custom-cut wig is shipped directly to them. Service is Girl on the Go!'s hallmark as Sheril hires top-notch cosmetologists who know the product and can help customers personalize their looks and bring their hair creations to life.

From the start, it was important to Sheril that Girl on the Go! be a business that gives back and she made that value part of her mission. For instance, she gave up the opportunity to earn rewards and other perks that credit cards companies offer to small business owners when they sign up for credit lines, choosing instead a Visa card that benefits St. Jude's Children's Research Hospital, one of the world's premier centers for research and treatment of catastrophic diseases, primarily cancer, in children. Sheril uses her St. Jude's card to purchase every wig she buys for a client because she likes the "karma" of spending money that in turn is contributed toward curing cancer or helping someone live with cancer.

Sheril also gives presentations titled "Wigs: Wear Them Well, The Emotional Journey of Hair Loss" for cancer non-profit organizations, wellness centers, and local hospitals. Rather than giving a sales pitch, Sheril approaches women in her audiences as an advocate and educator offering encouragement as they handle their baldness while their cancers go into remission. Her interactive sessions allow women to try on all types of wigs so they can appreciate and embrace the freedom of wearing a wig that makes them look and feel good.

Several feature stories about Sheril and Girl on the Go! have appeared in local and national media, including *Business Week, More, Star-Ledger* (Newark, New Jersey), *Times Union* (Albany, New York), *Daily News* (New York, New York), WABC-TV Channel 7 (New York, New York), NY1 Cable News, and "American Voices with Senator Bill Bradley" on Sirius Satellite Radio. Before launching Girl on the Go!, this alumnae of Boston University and The American University spent 10 years working for Fortune 500 companies in entertainment, healthcare, and banking, including NBC, American Express, JP Morgan Chase, and Oxford Health Plans. After 12 years of living in Manhattan, this girl on the go gave up the big city and is now living in upstate New York with her husband and two children.

Marketing comes second nature to Sheril, and she has put her knowledge and skills to work fearlessly promoting Girl on the Go!.

# Q&A with Sheril

**Q: What market research did you conduct to create and ultimately refine the concept for Girl on the Go!?**

A: Initially, I relied on my own experience because it felt like the right place to start. When I was diagnosed with cancer, I felt overwhelmed and frightened and I was also very worried about losing my hair. I felt strangely guilty for being concerned about my hair when my doctor was discussing my life. Yet, I could not stop thinking about how would I look without my beautiful waist-length hair. I worried that wearing a wig would make my illness stand out, turning a very private, personal experience into a "public outing."

I knew I had the inner and physical strength to fight my cancer, but I resented having to use some of that energy to fight for my privacy. The thought of finding and then walking into a wig shop made me feel as if I was "on display," sick, alone, and vulnerable. The salespeople I encountered rushed me and pushed me around, and they didn't want me to bring a friend along for advice. I started Girl on the Go! so others wouldn't go through the same experience.

I immersed myself in the wig business and met with wholesalers, retailers, and stylists in Brooklyn's [New York] wig district. I also spoke to women who wore wigs. I performed Internet searches and discovered that wig retail stores were not providing private consultations, which was critical because customers can get confused as wig prices range from $40 and $4,000.

I figured if Avon and Mary Kay could sell makeup through personal selling, then why wouldn't that same concept work for wigs? I hired four part-time stylists, each of whom had a personal connection to someone with cancer. They would bring our wig samples into people's homes and style them as the client liked. In mid-December 2003, my three oncologists placed Girl on the Go! brochures in their offices and I got my first client within a week. By the time my business became full-time in October 2004, I had helped 100 clients. Now, I'm setting up agreements with other women to expand into a handful of states.

---

**Q: The name "Girl on the Go!" appears to have a dual meaning for your business. How are you able to incorporate those meanings as you position your brand in customers' minds?**

A: The philosophy of Girl on the Go! speaks to the empowerment of our clients and how we want them to feel after they select the wig that's right for them. A fabulous wig empowers women in ways you can't imagine until you see it for yourself. A good wig preserves a woman's privacy – no one has to know she's even wearing one. Women don't have to suffer through the shame and stigma of losing their hair. They can be private about it and remain "on the go."

---

**Q: Girl on the Go! was a breakthrough concept for cancer patients who wanted a private alternative when shopping for wigs. What strategy did you use to introduce this unique concept to your target customers?**

A: I set out to re-engineer the wig shopping experience. I put the focus where it belongs, on the customer herself.

My work at JP Morgan Chase and American Express taught me that if you focus on the customer, great things happen. My consultants are coached and trained to emphasize the privacy of the shopping experience and to be supportive and compassionate during this difficult time for the customer. We approach each customer with integrity; they trust us to be there for them.

**Q: Who are your competitors and what do you do to stay ahead of them?**

A: My competitors are other online and retail wig stores. They don't have the same service model that we do. That's where we differ and how we stay ahead. We offer customers a unique, personal, and compassionate shopping experience.

**Q: You have successfully expanded Girl on the Go! beyond its geographical roots in New York and its cancer-patients origins to provide wigs and consultations to other women who desire high-quality wigs. How did these opportunities present themselves and what has been your strategy to capitalize on them? How do you keep from "overextending" the brand?**

A: Initially, I thought of providing our services to customers beyond cancer patients, but that wasn't a key focus for me. Soon after I launched the business, I started getting calls from people who were way outside of my geographic area – Pennsylvania, Massachusetts, and West Virginia. That's how the "Look Just Like You" concept was born.

I carefully manage the growth of my business and my brand. New York City and New Jersey are still the core geographies we serve, and I want to continue to grow organically. We have already expanded to California, Boston, and upstate New York. Eventually, I'll have an army of Girl on the Go! representatives across the country.

I hear from people daily who want to provide this service in their local communities. New territory takes hard work and commitment. Right now, "go slowly" is the name of the game.

**Q: What promotional campaign for your business has had the greatest impact on your sales? What was your least successful campaign?**

A: My most successful promotion has been internet search engine optimization because my customers do their initial research about wigs online, where they can privately evaluate different options. I hired a firm to help me place my business highly on search engine pages and it's working well.

Word of mouth has also played a critical role in my marketing strategy. Girl on the Go! is not the kind of business that people know about until they need it. It's not like you scribble down Girl on the Go!'s name to make yourself a note to check it out later. So I rely on my clients and their friends and families, doctors, and service providers to help me with spreading the word.

The least successful campaign involved directly targeting doctors and oncologists. In that space, I'm competing with established drug companies and service providers who spend big dollars to grab mindshare and influence doctors to recommend their products. Also, doctors and oncologists typically don't want to get involved in this type of personal transaction.

Before Girl on the Go! can really succeed, it needs to be an established brand. We're getting some wins here, being named to Oxford Health Plan's preferred providers list. But we still have work to do.

I haven't had much success with hiring PR firms to generate publicity for my business. They are expensive and can't guarantee that you'll get press coverage. Most of the publicity opportunities for Girl on the Go! have been created by myself or by a reporter contacting me directly after hearing about our service.

**Q: What advice would you give to fellow women entrepreneurs who are looking for that breakthrough marketing opportunity for their business?**

A: Be bright and creative. Talk about your business to everyone. Be willing to eat, sleep, and breathe your business. You have to be willing to just work it, girl, because no one is going to do for you!

*Learn more about Sheril and her company at*
*http://www.girlonthego.biz.*

CHAPTER 6: MARKETING THE BUSINESS

# CHAPTER 7

# THE ART OF NETWORKING

## GET TO THE RIGHT PEOPLE.

## BEYOND COLLECTING BUSINESS CARDS

As an entrepreneur, you can either view networking as a welcome opportunity to make new professional connections or avoid it until someone drags you to a local business event against your will. I'll bet any business cards you collected at the last chamber of commerce luncheon you attended are still hidden away in the corner of your desk drawer. Love it or hate it, networking is a necessary strategy for you to develop valuable relationships that ensure the success of your business.

Networking is a skill that comes naturally to women. Studies by the Center for Women's Business Research have shown that women emphasize relationship building as well as fact finding in their approach to managing their businesses and are more likely to consult with experts, employees, and fellow business owners about their businesses than their male counterparts.[16] However, women often do not have access to the types of networks that can help move a business forward. For instance, if you started your business without a lot of experience or contacts, you may find yourself struggling against an established male-dominated system of customers, suppliers, and creditors. Without the right contacts or support, it may be difficult to "crack the code" of the "good ol' boys' club."[17]

Despite obstacles like these, women entrepreneurs have to make their presence known by focusing their energy and time on developing high-value relationships with people who can help take their businesses to new heights. Over the past few years, more and more business groups, professional associations, and community organizations have jumped on the networking bandwagon by creating ongoing opportunities for members to meet in person at conferences, seminars, and events and virtually through online communities. The dizzying array of mailing lists and directories can make it difficult for a busy entrepreneur to pinpoint where and how to spend her precious time. You feel like a politician as you shake a lot of hands and collect business cards at these functions, and then you must endure incessant emails with sales pitches in hopes of meeting someone with a common interest who can really help move your business forward.

Networking should deliver results for you and your business. Here's how to get your networking strategy to work for you.

## IDENTIFY THE "NETWORKING OBJECTIVE"

Your life revolves around your business and the actions you take to implement new ideas, raise capital, acquire and satisfy customers, generate revenue, and control costs. Approach networking as you would any other activity designed to benefit your business. Identify the objective you want to accomplish through networking and ensure that objective aligns with what you're doing overall to drive your business. "Networking with a purpose" is what will deliver tangible results.

Suppose you're getting your idea off the ground and you're walking around with the business plan in your head. You know you need to create that formal business plan that we discussed in Chapter 3 and think it might be a good idea to network with successful entrepreneurs who can help you through the process. Translate that goal into a specific objective: Ask for a private meeting with the president of the local chamber of commerce to get his or her recommendations on small business owners with successful track records who want to mentor up-and-coming entrepreneurs. Creating a specific objective allows you to target the exact result you want without having to fight through a crowd at a networking event.

## BRING THE PEOPLE IN THE BACKGROUND TO THE FOREGROUND

Chances are you didn't build your business by yourself, and you're certainly not conducting business with just yourself. Every entrepreneur has people working in the background of their business – friends, family, investors, bankers, suppliers, customers, clients, employees, advisors, and mentors. You need to bring these people into the foreground when the time is right. In other words, you don't necessarily have to meet new people to make new connections because you probably already know someone who can assist with a problem you're trying to solve or an opportunity you're pursuing.

One of my dreams for Dessert Noir Café & Bar is to take the concept to the United Arab Emirates within the next few years. As I think about what it's going to take to make that vision a reality, I don't need to make cold calls to commercial leasing agents in Dubai or Abu Dhabi who wouldn't give a small business like mine the time of day. I already have key people in my network who can show me how to navigate that landscape, like a friend I've known since graduate school who works in banking in Riyadh, Saudi Arabia and does business throughout the Middle East.

## SEE AND BE SEEN

It makes perfect sense to join professional associations and business groups and attend their events, seminars, and conferences so people know you and your business are out there. That's why you tell the story about your business to anyone who will listen because you never know who might have something valuable that could give you and your business an edge in the marketplace.

Use this time wisely, though. Get creative and target people you know you want to meet. See if you can obtain a copy of the attendee list for an event you will be attending. These attendee lists will generally contain the names, titles, company names, and contact information of your fellow attendees, giving you extra intelligence to help you align your networking objective with the right people. Make it your intention to leave the event having met a handful of people who can make a difference in your business, not with a business card collection to add to your stack back at your desk.

As I noted in the chapter on marketing your business, successful entrepreneurs create visibility for their businesses and themselves as personalities by finding innovative, creative ways to keep the spotlight pointed in their direction and generate word of mouth. When you're perceived as an active member of the local business community, high-value networking opportunities will come to you.

The reality is that most of us are ordinary folks with no clout to grab headlines in the *New York Times* or the *Wall Street Journal*. Nevertheless, you have opportunities to partner with experts in your local community – e.g., authors, local luminaries, well-known business people, and non-profit organizations – and associate yourself and your business with the latest trends, news, and causes that complement your business strategy. Cultivating relationships with a few local reporters can also keep your name circulating when you have a new product to launch, an event to promote, or a cause to support. Think about all the ways that celebrities and big businesses keep their names in the papers. There's no reason why you can't use similar tactics. (Just make sure your role model is scandal-free!)

## LOOK FOR CONNECTIONS THAT MAY NOT BE OBVIOUS

You are already in tune with trends in the industry and subscribe to a number of news sources to keep up with the latest information. It's time to take your activities one step farther: Start paying attention and track the people who are quoted in articles, appear on news programs as experts, and speak publicly on your areas of interest. Don't be afraid to reach out to these people if there's common ground on which you could potentially build a mutually beneficial business relationship.

For example, the PR strategy for my business focuses on gener-ating positive press coverage with local media outlets, and I have successfully placed numerous stories with the major local newspapers, TV, radio stations, and online media. Recently, I began pitching my story to national media outlets to generate broad awareness for myself and my unique restaurant concept. This is no small task because I'm competing on a national scale with other businesses that are also vying for media attention.

With the help of a friend who has connections in the talk-show business, I created a package to send to producers of top-rated, nationally-televised shows who would potentially find my story compelling and newsworthy. Shortly after sending this package to one particular producer, I attended a conference where a panel discussion featured women entrepreneurs. Lisa Price, the founder of Carol's Daughter (you read her Q&A in Chapter 2), told the story of how she started her small business out of her home and eventually grew the company into a successful brand of beauty products. Along the way, a talk show producer discovered Lisa when she was showing her product line at a holiday event, and that producer contacted her to feature her story on the show. That TV appearance generated more interest in the national media and her business took off.

After the panel discussion, I made my way to the front of the room to introduce myself to Lisa and to share my experience about pitching national talk shows about my story. It turns out that the producer who discovered her was the same one to whom I sent the package about my business. With Lisa's help, my blind pitch, which had been sitting on the producer's desk for months, suddenly had a familiar name attached to it. When I contacted the producer again upon Lisa's recommendation, she returned my phone call.

On the surface, restaurants and beauty products don't seem to have much in common. I went into that panel discussion expecting nothing beyond the opportunity to hear the perspectives of successful women entrepreneurs. But my eyes and ears were open to the possibilities of creating new connections and forging new relationships. The act of stepping forward and introducing myself to Lisa created a new opportunity for my business.

# GIVE BACK

As with any relationship, there's an element of give and take that must occur for networking to work. If you are taking too much from your network, it won't be long before you are dropped to the bottom of your contacts' call-back lists. Think strategically about your network and the people who might naturally benefit from knowing one another, and don't hesitate to make those introductions. If you can create a high-value connection on someone else's behalf, it strengthens the network and ensures the success of all its members. Looking beyond your own needs and interests creates an atmosphere of "doing good unto others," which ultimately will reward you in small and large ways. Never let competitiveness drive you when you're dealing with your network.

When you have the opportunity to involve people in a high-profile activity or opportunity, think about the people in your network who would appreciate and benefit most from the opportunity. As I mentioned previously, I've created opportunities for Hollywood celebrities to dine at my restaurant in Beaverton, Oregon, a rare occurrence, to say the least. To accomplish this, I created a "short list" of people in my network who I wanted to make sure had a seat when those celebrities showed up at my restaurant. The goodwill that simple act created will last a lifetime.

## Divas Lesson #7
### It's not just who you know; it's who they are.

You meet people every day, but are you meeting the right people who can help you get great results for you and your business? When you clearly identify the objective you want to accomplish through your networking, analyze how to leverage your existing contacts, make yourself visible in the community, think broadly about opportunities, and look for ways to give back when you've been helped, the "right" people are well within your reach.

# NETWORKING:

## CRYSTAL MCCRARY ANTHONY
### Lawyer, Novelist, Film/TV Producer, and Commentator

To borrow from the late James Brown, Crystal McCrary Anthony has to be the "hardest working woman in show business." She has charted her own path in media and entertainment by playing to her strengths, following her instincts for what's hot in the marketplace, being a well-rounded expert, and leveraging her network to take advantage of highly visible, lucrative opportunities.

A native of Detroit who now makes her home in New York City, Crystal graduated *cum laude* with a double major in English and communications from the University of Michigan, Ann Arbor; went on to earn a law degree from New York University School of Law; and became barred in New York, where she practiced entertainment law specializing in theater production, publishing contracts, and director's agreements with the New York City firm of Paul, Weiss, Rifkind, Wharton, and Garrison.

Crystal left the law firm to pursue her passion for writing full time, contributing to several magazines, including *Vibe, Glamour, Savoy,* and *Tastemakers NYC,* and building on that experience to pen her best-selling novel, *Homecourt Advantage,* the story of a fictional NBA team's exploits both on and off the court and the struggle the players' wives and girlfriends endure to maintain a level of sanity and normalcy amidst the temptations of fame, fortune, and infidelity. (Something Crystal knows about firsthand having been married previously to New York Knicks star player Greg Anthony for several years.) The Literary Guild recognized *Homecourt Advantage* as a featured alternate selection, and Sony/Screen Gem bought the rights to bring the story to the silver screen. Crystal's second published novel, *Gotham Diaries*, was a *New York Times* bestseller and was named the 2005 Blackboard Fiction Book of the Year.

Today, Crystal is the executive producer of two new television shows on BET-J: "Real Life Divas," which profiles African-American women who have shaped our culture artistically, socially, and politically, and "My Model Looks Better than Your Model," which is hosted by "America's Next Top Model" winner Eva Pigford. Crystal is also the executive producer of the independent film *Dirty Laundry*, the American Black Film Festival's Best Feature Film winner starring Loretta Devine, Rockmond Dunbar, Jenifer Lewis, Terri J. Vaughn, Sommore, and Maurice Jamal. Finally, she has appeared as a regular pop culture critic on CNN's *American Morning*; has been a legal analyst on numerous television networks, including Fox News, CNBC and Court TV; and is the co-host of BET-J's "My Two Cents."

Being outspoken on women's issues, literacy, children's rights, and race, Crystal definitely generates buzz. She has appeared on several national television shows, including "Good Morning, America;" "Access Hollywood;" "Extra;" and "The Tavis Smiley Show;" and has been featured in *Newsweek, New York Times, Mirabella, Essence, O: The Oprah Magazine, People, Sister-to-Sister, New York Daily News,* and *USA Today.*

Despite her busy schedule, this mother of two young children still finds time to give back to her community. Crystal serves on the advisory board of Jumpstart, a national organization dedicated to increasing early childhood literacy particularly in low-income neighborhoods across the country, and on the advisory committee of Hyperion Books' Voice imprint, which specifically focuses on women in their mid-30s and offers books that answer today's women's needs. Crystal has got to "feel good!" Hit me!

# Q&A with Crystal

**Q: The success of your next film or TV project heavily depends on your networking with the right people. How do you approach networking for your business?**

A: You always hear from experts and professionals about the importance of networking. Obviously, it's a pivotal component of any successful career, whether you're in Corporate America, Wall Street, or entertainment. I don't think of myself as a great networker who can go into a situation cold, come out with a business card, and automatically have that turn into something.

My approach to networking is organic. I am building on the relationships I've built over the last 20 years. I put myself in the right place at the right time, align myself with people who share my interests, and see what happens. I attend film festivals and go to book signings of authors who interest and appeal to me. I make sure that I attend events and parties with a specific networking goal in mind.

For example, when I practiced entertainment law at Paul, Weiss, Rifkind, Wharton, and Garrison, I knew law wasn't part of my long-term plan. Eventually, I began to seriously plan the next steps toward developing my writing career. After writing my first book, which I optioned to be made into a film, I ran into a former law colleague who had accepted a position with Miramax. Although my film was never made, I expressed to him my continued interest in film. A few years later, I heard that he was working as a seller of films. When I was assembling my team of key business partners for *Dirty Laundry,* I reconnected with him.

**Q: As a well-known woman in media and entertainment, how have you broken through the "good 'ol boy clubs" within the industry?**

A: I don't think I've broken through. I think I've just let my work speak for itself. I take on projects – books, TV shows, or films – that are meaningful to me and execute them with great quality, integrity, and professionalism. I strive for excellence and have an incredible eye for detail, always mindful of a certain truth I want to come across in my work and never dumbing down any of my characters. I surround myself with great people – writing partners, lawyers, assistants, producers, etc. – who help me get the job done and believe in my vision and the stories I want to tell.

African-American women are told that they have to work twice as hard for their success. I cannot speak for other people about how hard they are working, but I know this has always been true for me. I believe in the "Big P": Perseverance. If you are determined and work toward your goals, if you get a little luck and good karma along the way, you will be successful.

---

## Q: How have your board positions helped you?

A: My board positions serve as the barometer for what's really important in my life. This works helps my heart, nurtures my spirits, and puts me in touch with my humanity.

With Jumpstart, I'm passionate about educating the next generation. These children are languishing in a public school system that's woefully inadequate and failing so many children. Literacy is the key that unlocks the world to education. I can relate to these children's experiences because I didn't learn to read until I was in the fourth grade.

I'm very excited about the opportunity to serve on the advisory committee of Voice, the imprint from Hyperion Books that focuses on publishing books for women. There is an impressive roster of women business and cultural leaders who recognize the need for an outlet that's dedicated to offering books that answer the needs of today's women's. What I bring to this committee is the young African-American perspective, representing an audience that's been traditionally underserved by mainstream publishers and emerging as a force of inspiration and knowledge for all women, whether they are of color or not.

**Q: We spend a lot of time networking because we want access to influential people who can help move us forward, but you just never know when or how you're going to meet them. How do you ensure you're prepared?**

A: I believe that if you're meeting someone to make something happen, you are putting the cart before the horse. When I was struggling with my decision to become a full-time writer, I called upon a girlfriend and shared my frustrations. I thought if I could get all these people I knew to help me with what I wanted to do, then everything would fall into place. My friend was a TV writer in Los Angeles and she shared with me a brilliant quote from her manager who went on to a lucrative career in TV and film: "The second I stopped trying to depend on the people around me to 'hook me up' and started creating and doing my work myself, that's when I really started to succeed."

If all your ducks are in a row and you're making things happen on your own, then you've positioned yourself to succeed. People will come to you. All the relationships I've developed came about because I was prepared and I created something for the larger universe that someone else valued. Be prepared, focused, and strategic and have a plan in place to achieve your goal. Be passionate and persistent.

---

**Q: Networking relationships are give and take and it's important that you're not always perceived as a "taker." How have you given back to the people in your network?**

A: It's important to not always be a "taker." I'm very familiar with that type of person, the one who's always hording all the knowledge, contacts, and information, particularly in the entertainment business where people "eat their young."

From the smallest thing to the biggest thing, I've prided myself on giving back in a variety of ways. I believe in the old saying, "To whom much is given much is expected." I want to share my knowledge with other people. I want to make referrals. I want to open a door that will give someone else an opportunity to succeed. The light from your single candle can illuminate the entire network.

*Learn more about Crystal and her company at http://www.crystalmccraryanthony.com.*

# CHAPTER 8

# KINDNESS AND COMPASSION HAVE A PLACE IN BUSINESS

## GIVING BACK.

## EVERYBODY'S LOOKING FOR A HAND

According to a study by the Center for Women's Business Research, nine out of 10 business owners contribute money to charities, far surpassing the rate of the general population, and women entrepreneurs are more likely to take on leadership roles when they volunteer for non-profit organizations.[18]

Knowing that you're already likely to support them, a vast array of non-profits, booster clubs, school fundraising committees, and charitable organizations with worthy causes in your local community will ask you to donate to their causes or volunteer your time if you have a visible retail storefront, office building, or work site where you can be found. In most cases, when you register for a business license or join your local chamber of commerce, you'll get hit before you even open your doors because your company's name and contact information will be out there for all to see. And when the word gets out that you've supported a cause or contributed to a charity, even more folks will come crawling out of the woodwork.

Since Dessert Noir Café & Bar has received steady press coverage and is well-known in the community, the restaurant is a popular choice for community organizations. We get hit several times a month with requests for free food or gift certificates for auctions, special events, and other fundraising activities. With this many requests, it is impossible for us to support everyone who asks for help.

As with all aspects of your operation, when it comes to aligning your business with a charitable cause, you need to think strategically. Align your philanthropy with your business objectives. Clearly outline your expectations with each charitable organization before agreeing to donate your time, money, product, or service to support their cause. I have developed these criteria to assess opportunities to support local community causes and organizations:

## 1. Does the request align with the causes and issues I personally advocate and support?

Causes that I am passionate about include underprivileged children and families, education, providing safe haven and care for animals in need, finding cures for diseases, protecting women's rights, and supporting relief efforts for victims of natural and man-made disasters.

## 2. Are the people in this organization already supporting my business?

When I receive letters, emails, or phone calls from people looking for a donation, they almost always get my attention if they personalize the correspondence and start by saying, "I'm one of your customers and my friends and family love your place and come in all the time." Form letters and mass mailings almost always get tossed into the trash, even if the cause is one I support.

## 3. Are there opportunities to promote my business to a large number of people?

For fundraising events, organizations will often create flyers, programs, and other marketing materials where they advertise the names of their supporters. These pieces usually have life beyond the day of the event as keepsakes and souvenirs. There may also be opportunities to participate in the event itself, such as speaking to the audience for a few minutes about the business.

## 4. Have I contributed to this organization before and did I see results?

History with an organization is a good predictor of future donations. If the organization helped promote my business and I gained new customers as a result, then I'll continue to support it.

## 5. Can I get a tax write-off?

You can't ignore the tax benefits of contributing to non-profit organizations. While many of your donations will be made "in kind" and won't be cash out of your pocket, it still costs you money to give away your product or service. You'll be able to declare the cash value of that contribution on your tax return. (Be sure to consult with your tax advisor about your specific situation when it comes to tax-deductible contributions.)

# THE CELEBRITY CHARITY EVENT – THE CAUSE AND YOUR BUSINESS IN THE SPOTLIGHT

I'm often asked, "How in the world did you get Morgan Freeman to come to Beaverton, Oregon?" As I described in the chapter on networking, when you think broadly and strategically about your network and devise ways to create visibility for your business, you generate connections and foster innovative ideas to keep the spotlight pointed in your direction, encourage positive word of mouth, and publicize your support of causes and issues that matter to you. I created the perfect opportunity to collaborate with Morgan by providing my business as a platform to raise awareness and funds for a worthy cause.

I first met Morgan in July 2006 in my role as the marketing and communications manager for Corporate Diversity at Intel Corporation. In that job, I drove our external engagement strategy with multi-cultural organizations, and as part of that strategy, the company participated in several conferences and events each year. We organized a highly-visible presence around Intel's Digital Home technology at the National Urban League's conference in Atlanta, and Morgan joined our Intel executives for a presentation that highlighted ClickStar, Inc., the digital entertainment venture between Intel and Revelations Entertainment, the production company that Morgan heads with his business partner Lori McCreary.

Because my team was going crazy keeping up with everything we were doing on site – technology demonstrations, speaking points for our executives, audio/visual requirements, and the like – they did not have the bandwidth, patience, or interest to handle our celebrity spokesperson and all the numerous additional tasks that came with that responsibility. So they looked to me to take care of Morgan and be his "personal assistant for the day."

Morgan and I instantly established a rapport. At 72 years old, he's tall, fit, and handsome as well as warm, friendly, funny, wise, insightful, and straightforward. He's exactly how you would imagine him based on the characters he plays on screen.

Thrown together, we were two people with Southern roots breaking bread over grits and eggs at the Ritz-Carlton Hotel in downtown Atlanta. Our conversation revolved around a wide range of topics, including the fact that we're both restaurant owners. As luck would have it, his next movie project was bringing him to Portland, Oregon. After all was said and done in Atlanta, I hosted Morgan and his crew for dinner at my restaurant while he was in town, which created a lot of buzz for Dessert Noir Café & Bar.

Several weeks after Morgan's visit to Portland, I caught an interview with him on *The Oprah Winfrey Show* and couldn't believe what I saw: He and Oprah were doing a cooking demonstration with a celebrity chef from a restaurant in Los Angeles to promote his cookbook, *Morgan Freeman and Friends: Caribbean Cooking for a Cause*, the sales proceeds from which would go to the Grenada Relief Fund (GRF), an organization he co-founded and has been actively supporting since Hurricanes Ivan and Emily devastated the island of Grenada in 2004 and 2005, respectively. Since then, GRF has changed its name to PLAN!T NOW and expanded its scope to include victims of natural and manmade disasters in other Caribbean nations as well as the Gulf States in the United States.

My first thought was, "I spent several hours talking to Morgan about everything under the sun, and this cookbook never came up!" Watching him on TV inspired me to think about how I could support his efforts, and I contacted him with a brilliant idea:

Because Dessert Noir Café & Bar is located next to a Century Theatres multiplex, I proposed a special screening of one of his latest movies, where local audiences would interact with him directly in short question-and-answer sessions. Later in the day, Dessert Noir Café & Bar would host a Caribbean-themed VIP reception and party. Finally, we would hold an evening event at a venue in downtown Portland to bring out a large crowd in support of the cause. All of the proceeds from the various events would be donated to PLAN!T NOW.

Morgan loved the idea and put me in touch with his team to make it happen. However, when you're working with celebrities, you learn quickly that their time is fluid. Their lives are hectic and fast-paced and commitments change all the time. One minute, the date for your event is confirmed, and the next you are reworking your calendar because your event got bumped for a higher-priority gig.

Therefore, remaining flexible is critical. Here we are more than two years later and we're still working on securing the date for our charity event. Yes, Morgan still thinks it's a good idea, but his calendar has been jam-packed with film commitments, appearances, special projects, family priorities, and other activities that have taken precedent. Not to mention that Morgan was in a serious car accident in August 2008, which forced a lot of delays to many of his projects, not just my event in Oregon. So I've had to revise, reconsider, and relax the time-critical aspects of the events to ensure it would remain fresh, newsworthy, and exciting. (I'm hoping for a date in the fall of 2009.)

The appearance of an Oscar-winning actor in the Portland area doesn't occur very often. I have an opportunity to use Morgan's upcoming appearance as a way to combat the climate of "bad news" that experts predict will be with us throughout 2009 – local company cutbacks and job losses, government budget deficits, fallout from the sub-prime mortgage crisis, tightening of the credit markets, ongoing wars in Iraq and Afghanistan, you name it. Here's a chance to rally our local community around something positive to help people in need. With the support of sponsors, donors, and volunteers, including a local TV station that has agreed to provide broadcast advertising and publicity, I know I can create a memorable event for our community, one that people would talk about for years to come.

## Divas Lesson #8
## Be kind and compassionate and more business will come your way.

Milton Hershey, the founder of Hershey Foods, once wrote, "One is only happy in proportion as he makes others feel happy, and only useful as he contributes his influences for the finer callings in life." As entrepreneurs, we experience many trials in running our businesses, but that should not prevent us from giving back to our communities. Supporting charitable causes and organizations that align with your strategy makes good business sense because it allows you to increase your visibility and stature in the community, create a positive perception with your customers and supporters, and build a reputation for being a good corporate citizen.

# KINDNESS AND COMPASSION:

## VALERIE RED-HORSE
### Red-Horse Native Productions and Tribal Finance/ Asset Management for Western International Securities, Inc.

The Cherokee Nation has an old saying: "When you were born, you cried and the world rejoiced. Live your life so that when you die, the world cries and you rejoice." As an accomplished investment banker, filmmaker, entrepreneur, wife, and mother, Valerie Red-Horse is one Cherokee who takes this saying to heart.

After founding and serving as the chairman, CEO, and majority shareholder of Red-Horse Securities, LLC (formerly Native Nations Securities), believed to be the country's first Native American investment bank, Valerie now heads the Tribal Finance Division and Tribal Asset Management Division of Western International Securities. This veteran of Drexel Burnham Lambert has led over 50 financing deals totaling over $2 billion and works with tribal nations throughout North America to provide them with financing and economic development resources for gaming, infrastructure, and long-term financial planning.

Valerie is best known for her tireless work to bring accurate stories and portrayals of Native Americans to television and film. (Little known fact: Valerie was the model for Mattel's Pocahontas doll, which was inspired by the 1995 Disney film). In 1995, her feature screenplay *Lozen*, the true story of an Apache woman warrior, was selected for the prestigious Sundance Institute's Writers Lab. A year later, Valerie launched Red-Horse Native Productions, whose first project was *Naturally Native*, an independent feature film that she wrote, produced, co-directed, starred, and distributed. That film premiered at the 1998 Sundance Film Festival and secured a U.S. theatrical release. Valerie also has written and produced several documentaries, including the award-winning PBS production *True Whispers*, which chronicles the story of the Navajo Code Talkers, and her project for the Choctaw Nation about the tribe's involvement and contributions to World War I.

A *cum laude* graduate of the film and theater program at the University of California at Los Angeles, Valerie is the founder of the Hollywood Access Program for Natives (HAPN), a non-profit educational and training organization for Native American youth who are interested in the entertainment business. A sought-after expert whose story and perspectives have appeared in several publications, including the *Wall Street Journal, Fortune Small Business,* and *Minority Business Entrepreneur,* Valerie received the 2007 Legacy of Leadership Award from Spelman College and is a current member of the Directors Guild of America and the Screen Actors Guild. Valerie lives in southern California with her husband of 28 years, former NFL football player, Curt Mohl, with whom she has three children ages 25, 21, and 12.

## Q&A with Valerie

**Q: Given the range of Native American causes and organizations and the great need for assistance among many Native people, how do you determine which organizations to support? How do you align your philanthropy with the goals and strategies of your business?**

A: I happen to be a Christian believer, and though I would never assert my personal values and choices on anyone else, being a Christian guides everything I do. I dedicate a minimum percentage of my income to "God's work," and that contribution can be small or large depending on my role.

I tend to stay away from the big causes and organizations that are already getting a lot of attention and resources. Instead, I focus on defining a need and determining how I can use my influence, skills, and knowledge to advance a cause in the community.

For example, I was working on a financing deal for a tribe in Minnesota to build a new administrative building. This is an area that's extremely depressed and hurting for development. There's misinformation about how government services are administered on reservations, and you'll find that the truth is there is not enough money in the community to fund basic government services. Citizens of this tribe lacked access to healthcare; they were unable to secure transportation to cities off the reservation; and unemployment was high. Elders could not afford to heat their homes, and children were not getting the basic healthcare they needed.

It was obvious that this was a community in crisis. To help this community, I used money from my fund for "God's Work" and started a ministry through my church. Our church was already providing aid in Third World countries around the world. I convinced them to support this community right here in the United States. We brought in medical experts and volunteers to assist in providing health care at clinics, repairing dilapidated homes, and setting up children's programs. Now we're looking to expand our efforts to other tribal nations located on reservations.

It's exciting to be the spark that started something. I looked at what I could provide beyond the simple act of financing an administrative building and engaged my network to assist a community in need.

---

**Q: You have spent your career identifying business ventures that not only create opportunities for your own personal success, but also address a specific need in the Native American community, including film/TV production, advertising, beauty products, and your latest venture in investment banking and finance. How are you able to harness your vision when other companies have failed to see this market's potential?**

A: I don't think other companies have failed to see the potential. They're just looking at commercial interests and opportunities. They absolutely recognize, for example, that the Native American gaming industry hit an all-time high of $26 billion in 2007. In entertainment, a large cable network recently produced a critically-acclaimed film which featured a well-known historic Native storyline and Native American talent and had great production value. But Hollywood tends to do films "about" us and not "of" us. This film lacked the sensibility of coming from the community because there were not any writers, directors, or producers who were "above the line." Contrast that with my productions where I go into the Native American community and work with the elders and the tribal people to develop the content, the story, the portrayals, and the history.

It's all in the approach. I'm building relationships, understanding the community I'm working in, and I'm committed to being in it for the long term. That's what I bring to the table – knowledge and understanding to go beyond exploiting commercial interests. Just because my projects are not motivated solely by commercial interests doesn't mean that my projects can't be commercially successful. Anything we do must be sustainable and meaningful and have a positive impact on the next generation of Native people.

---

**Q: Where do you believe you've had the greatest impact in making a difference in the lives of Native American people? Where do you think you have more to do?**

A: In my work, I invest a lot of time to improve opportunities in education. I founded a non-profit organization promoting education for Native people in the entertainment industry. Ancestrally, training and education have always been important in our community. We often lose sight of the value of handing down knowledge. Witness how teachers are among the lowest paid professionals in this country and parents aren't taking an active interest in their children's education. I feel a tremendous responsibility to add to the legacy of training and education by being a good educator and mentor.

I want to do more to encourage and empower our youth. Every day I wake up excited about the day. I want to see more of our kids have that same energy and excitement. Tradition and culture are lifelines in the Native community, and we have to pass these beliefs on to our kids.

**Q: Do women entrepreneurs have a responsibility to contribute to the communities in which we operate our businesses?**

A: Society puts a lot of responsibility on women. We are givers of life; we are nurturers and caregivers. When we step out as entrepreneurs, it is perceived as cutting edge. This perception is magnified when you are a minority.

We have to understand that we are also role models. Be a role model and do your best. It's too easy to just to do your own thing. Leave a legacy you can feel good about. My children are my greatest legacy.

**Q: What advice would you offer to an entrepreneur who is struggling to find a way to give back to her community when she barely has the time and energy to run her business?**

A: There's a reason why the safety procedures on an airplane direct you to apply your own oxygen mask first before helping someone else. As women, we take care of everything and everybody and risk being no good to either. Take care of yourself and you'll find the way – through your time, your energy, and your mentoring. If you're bogged down and overworked, you can't be any good to anyone else.

**Q: Oprah Winfrey once said, "If you seek what is honorable, what is good, what is the truth of your life, all the other things you could not imagine will come as a matter of course." How are you putting this idea into practice in your own life and your business?**

A: That's very interesting. In fact, that quote paraphrases the Bible, specifically Matthew 5:33. It's really His work that I want to do. It's not my goal to be selfish or to make the most money. I have an amazing marriage to a man I've been with for 28 years, three great children, businesses, films. I strive for balance and could never achieve it if I didn't live God's plan.

## Q: What's on the horizon?

A: I'm working to educate women entrepreneurs about the financial options that exist in the investment banking space. A variety of financial tools exist that traditionally have not been available to women entrepreneurs in the past. Women need education and support on the differences between investment banks and commercial banks.

*Learn more about Valerie and her company at http://www.valerieredhorse.com.*

# CHAPTER 9

# THE VALUE OF MAKING MISTAKES

## LEARNING IS A LIFELONG PURSUIT.

## "FAVORITE" MISTAKES

Entrepreneurs are often asked about their "favorite mistakes," lessons they learned that changed their lives or the course of their businesses. These are not the types of mistakes that you simply go through a minor course correction and you're back on track. No, we're talking about events that fundamentally change how you conduct business. Here's my example.

There is nothing like the experience of getting sued to make you pay close attention to the deficiencies in your operation. When you consider that Dessert Noir Café & Bar is a small, 60-seat, single-location restaurant, I really had no business sourcing my product from multi-million dollar food corporations, but I didn't know any better. Everyone who advised me about getting product for my business pointed me in the direction of the big corporations, and considering that I was consulting with so-called "experts," including my own management team and other restaurant owners, I trusted their experience and didn't question their advice. Let's call this "Mistake #1."

Big food corporations come with a lot of overhead – sales forces, delivery trucks, partner marketing programs, software for tracking orders, etc. Needless to say, someone has to pay for all this, and

I became concerned about how much we were spending on food deliveries. It's not unusual for costs to rise when you open a new business, and this is to be expected to some degree if you are also "learning as you go." However, we were just becoming established and I had no tolerance for overspending on food.

I had collected industry benchmarks and anecdotal data from other owners that reinforced my concerns that we were spending too much in relation to the business we were doing. I asked my sales representatives to investigate these issues and help me understand why we were buying so much from them when we didn't have the sales revenue to justify it. As you might imagine, this was like asking the fox to watch the henhouse. Let's call this "Mistake #2."

In the spring of 2006, the economy in the Portland area hit a bump in the road when several key environmental factors came into play over the course of two months – Spring Break (families were flat broke after taking their vacations), Easter and taxes landed on the same weekend (my restaurant could not compete with God and the government as people made their obligatory appearances at church on Sunday morning and spent the rest of the day in front of their PCs with TurboTax), and a significant spike in gas prices (SUV drivers put their cash into their gas tanks, leaving little money left for discretionary spending).

With these negative factors in the market, several popular, long-established, nationally-recognized restaurants went out of business or scaled down and reorganized. It was a miracle that Dessert Noir Café & Bar survived, for we suffered a greater than 20 percent decline in the first month of this cycle and it took another two months to return to our previous sales volume.

I had to "figure out" how to make payroll and meet my obligations for the business. Consequently, I fell behind on the payments on my food bill.

I worked with the company to keep my account in good standing and used the strategy of "they'd rather get paid late than not at all." But eventually I couldn't keep up, and my account was on its way to "bad debt land." Let's call this "Mistake #3."

I negotiated in good faith with the food company's credit department and worked out a payment schedule that would bring the account back into compliance. I asked the credit manager to allow me to place cash-on-delivery (COD) orders should the need arise. She agreed, we put the payment plan in writing, and I began working to pay the bills and get back on track.

Upon reviewing the entire financial picture for my business, I concluded that we needed to focus exclusively on repaying the debt – and not place orders – so I would not continue to add money to the outstanding balance. I quickly realized that when it came to food, I had options beyond relying on deliveries from a big food company. We could shop at farmers' markets, small wholesale distributors who cater to smaller restaurants, friends' backyard gardens, and even grocery stores in some cases, all of which offered much better food quality and prices.

When I told my sales director that I would no longer place food orders until our debt was repaid, he informed the credit manager, who reneged on our agreement and immediately reported the debt to a collections agency. I did not even have the opportunity to make the first payment in accordance with our agreement.

From there, I went through a miserable period in "collections hell," dealing with the repercussions of negative reporting to the credit bureaus and its effect on my ability to secure future financing, hiring attorneys to defend my company, and going through the lengthy litigation process. Eventually, we settled out of court, but the whole experience was a nightmare.

Believe it or not, this was a $25,000 mistake that kept me in business. In some cases, a mistake of this magnitude could potentially put an entrepreneur out of business. It forced me to dig deeper into my operation and demand more efficiencies and accountability from my employees. Because we had no credit with a food company, we were forced to pay COD for everything, which meant we had to be "lean and mean" about inventory management. We could no longer hide behind aging invoices. We began to manage our food and beverage inventory on a daily basis and instantly realized a decrease in our expenses when I got proactive and demanded that we only buy what we needed and no more. I've joked with my staff that even if Dessert Noir Café & Bar grows to 100 locations, we will still purchase our food ourselves everyday.

Of course, I wish I hadn't learned this lesson the hard way, but I'm glad I did, for Dessert Noir Café & Bar is a healthier, stronger operation as a result.

## Divas Lesson #9
### I live, I learn, I move on

Upon describing the process for creating his music, Russian composer Igor Stravinsky said, "I have learned throughout my life as a composer chiefly through my mistakes and pursuits of false assumptions, not by my exposure to founts of wisdom and knowledge." In short, we stand to learn the most when we've screwed up.

When we're executing our plans and giving ourselves entirely to the business, it's possible to lose sight of how the possibilities of making a mistake or taking an unexpected detour in our plan can provide insight and lessons to make yourself and your business stronger. Fear of failure and feelings of inadequacy, guilt, and shame may even play a role as we do our best to appear perfect and self-assured.

At one time or another, every entrepreneur has pursued a path or made a decision that didn't go exactly as hoped or planned. Use that moment to pull yourself out of the day-to-day grind and create a quiet space in your mind where you can hear what your inner voice is saying to you. Seek the advice of others you trust – especially those who have a contrarian perspective – to help you see the situation clearly. Allow them to offer alternatives for you to consider.

Accept the "gift" of a hard lesson with humility. Use it as an opportunity to stop and listen to yourself. Think about what that lesson might teach you. Appreciate and celebrate the insight you've gained and challenge yourself to apply what you've learned, pick yourself up, and move on to the next challenge.

# LEARNING FROM MISTAKES:

## JACQUELINE RHINEHART
### Organic Soul Marketing

While taking a journalism class at the University of South Carolina, Jacqueline Rhinehart was given a familiar assignment, writing her own obituary. She now recalls writing that the "deceased" Jacqueline Rhinehart had been a vice president of marketing at Warner Brothers Records. Well, the young college student wasn't too far off.

Combining her passion for music with a talent for connecting artists with their audiences, Jacqueline spent 20 years as a marketing and public relations executive in the music business working with some of the biggest R&B and hip hop artists of our time – Dionne Warwick, Aretha Franklin, Whitney Houston, Toni Braxton, TLC, NotoriousB.I.G., Sean "P. Diddy" Combs, L.A. Reid and Babyface, Mary J. Blige, Vanessa Williams, Nelly, Erykah Badu, Boys II Men, MasterP, to name a few.

Before striking out on her own in 1999 to co-found Organic Soul Marketing, a full-service marketing firm specializing in the launch and re-introduction of new entertainment products and services, Jacqueline worked for eight years as the senior vice president for marketing at Universal Records, which included the legendary Motown Records label. Carving out new territory for promoting urban music to the masses, Jacqueline was the force behind multi-million dollar advertising and media campaigns and highly visible cross-promotional ventures among Universal artists and companies such as Coca-Cola, Budweiser, and Black Entertainment Television. We take for granted today's 24/7, oversaturated media environment. Back then, Jacqueline was among the first to approach music promotions holistically, creating packages that developed avenues into all media outlets, including music videos, print, television, and radio campaigns, to create maximum visibility and exposure for her artists.

Before making her mark at Universal, Jacqueline served as senior director of publicity for Arista Records during the term of the legendary Clive Davis. At Arista, Jacqueline helped introduce LaFace Records with hit makers L.A. Reid and Babyface and created campaigns for the launch of Bad Boy Records and the *Waiting to Exhale* and *Preacher's Wife* soundtracks. Jacqueline also worked in marketing, publicity, and artist development roles for Uptown Records, Hiram Hicks Management, Mercury Records, and Hush Productions.

Entrepreneurship is nothing new to Jacqueline. In the early days of her career while she was still living in South Carolina, she started a small consulting firm called Jackie Productions/Tryad Services, which provided local marketing services for major labels whose artists needed a local presence. The firm booked Carolina bands into local venues and created street marketing and merchandising campaigns for record companies that did not have local offices. A fan of the late R&B superstar Rick James, she even developed his first line of T-shirts.

With nearly 30 years of experience under her belt, Jacqueline has experienced the ups and downs of being a woman with vision who is charting a new course in untested waters. Her new book, *My Organic Soul,* is all about discovery, renewal, and growth. She's made a few mistakes along the way, but they have not held her back from achieving her goals.

## Q&A with Jacqueline

**Q: As an entrepreneur, what mistake has taught you the greatest lesson? What did you learn from it?**

A: PRICING! I've learned that pricing is very important, and there is a fine line where you gauge what is appropriate to secure the business and not negate the value of the talent your price represents.

Funding is also very important, i.e., having the resources to go the distance in regard to investing in my business and seeing it to fruition.

---

## Q: How do you learn from your mistakes and apply the insight and knowledge you've gained toward improving your business?

A: First, I try not to become so discouraged by the process and the reaction of others. I sing the words of my favorite rap mantra and realize it's not the priority or compulsion of others to make things happen for me: "It's mine and God's; so I have to remain self-propelled, welcome and appreciate (really) the help you do receive." Keeping that calming thought helps me gain perspective, and the lessons and insights derived from the experience become obvious to me. From there, I remind myself of the lesson when needed. I recall it. I keep a journal of my journey.

I also tell myself, "Remember, child, you are not your emotions." Let your emotions come and go because they cannot and do not permanently define you unless you choose to hold on to them. If that's the case, you are free to act like a fool today and be a sage tomorrow. There is a permanent "you" that is unchanging and has nothing to do with the mistakes you've made or what things "look like today." Don't be afraid to say or do something just because you don't want to appear wrong. If you're wrong, you can always change your mind and be gracious about it!

---

## Q: From whom do you seek advice and counsel when you find the path you're on may be heading in the wrong direction?

A: I try to keep and develop my own counsel. This is a good habit to develop. Seek to know yourself and talk to God. I also seek counsel from those who are God's disciples. It is very good to talk to someone whose values are the same and more matured than your own. People may have different points of view, but they should share the greater moral compass.

**Q: When other women entrepreneurs approach you for guidance and mentoring about mistakes they've made in their businesses, how do you advise them to get back on track?**

A: Once they know their product is the best that it can be, or it's the best they SAY it is, then they simply must get back in the stream. Great ideas, products, and services will succeed simply because they are better. But the key comes in remaining in the game, not self-destructing. Think of all the great ones who committed suicide on purpose or by accident in the arts, in business, or in life. Think of those who stopped just short of their breakthrough, allowing some other business to reach their goal instead. Think of those who DO MAKE IT HAPPEN at whatever age – 40, 50, 60, 70, 80, or 90. They are a testament to the reality that the only impediment to your destiny is you because everything else rolls away if you outlive it!

*Learn more about Jacqueline and her company at http://www.jacquelinerhinehart.com.*

# CHAPTER 10

# BRINGING IT HOME

## THE LAST WORD.

## YOUR SENSE OF PURPOSE

Winston Churchill said, "If you're going through hell, keep going." Our journey as women entrepreneurs can be a long, difficult one, and going through hell is not fun or easy when you have cash flow challenges, employee relations issues, vendor management concerns, and the like.

You may think you're not going to make it. There will be days when you ask, "Exactly why did I do this to myself?" The stress and anxiety will keep you awake at night because you carry a burden that most people cannot appreciate or understand. Time and again, you will feel alone, helpless, depressed, incompetent, unmotivated, sick, and tired.

Your ultimate purpose is the light that will illuminate the path when you are too overwhelmed to see it. When you focus on your purpose, your inspiration for being in business in the first place, and stay true to your dream of success, the day-to-day trials and tribulations will become easier to manage. I live by this philosophy: God does not give me any more than I can handle, and when I wake up in the morning, I express my gratitude to Him and those who've helped me along the way. I ask for the strength and guidance to make good decisions and face challenges without fear or lack of faith and confidence. I can only pay one bill at a time, solve one problem at a time, address one issue at time. Reminding myself of these things prevents me from feeling powerless when the "going through hell" part of entrepreneurship gets way too hot.

## GET OUT OF THE WAY AND GET AWAY

I know now that sometimes I need to get out of my own way and let situations run their own course without intervention or direct action on my part. As entrepreneurs, it's natural to want to be extremely hands on. Some of us might even be "control freaks" who are constantly reviewing plans and strategies, coming up with new ideas, and getting ahead of the curve. When you're right there in the thick of it, there's always something you can or should be doing for the business.

It's healthy, though, to back off a bit and let the business "breathe" on its own without so much "life support." Give yourself a break, allow your team to demonstrate that they're capable of performing to your expectations, and trust yourself that the business is exactly where it needs to be right now, regardless of what else may be happening.

Not only do I advocate getting out of your own way, but I also highly recommend literally *getting away*. Once or twice a quarter, I take a trip out of town to escape the craziness of the day-to-day struggles and challenges so I can think strategically about the big picture. I choose places with vibrant local communities, great restaurants, and upscale evening entertainment where I can hang out with my friends and get ideas and inspiration for my own business. A few of my favorite locations: London, New York City, Las Vegas, Phoenix, San Francisco, Seattle, and Washington, D.C. Some of my best ideas have come to me when I'm on one of these trips because I'm in a completely different frame of mind and can brainstorm without feeling the constraints and demands of my real life.

## KNOWING WHEN IT'S TIME TO MOVE ON OR KEEP GOING

Eventually, you will approach the edge of the pre-determined boundaries protecting and balancing your M Factors. You will have to decide if it's best for you to keep going or if it's time to tell yourself, "I did my best and I'm done." The failure of your business does not mean you're a failure as an individual. Even if you fall flat on your face, that's forward motion, progress, an opportunity to learn. Chances are you'll take that experience and parlay it into your next entrepreneurial venture, approaching the new opportunity as a much smarter, wiser person who will know exactly what it will take to be successful.

In reviewing the exit strategy for my business, I reflected on the entire experience of owning this restaurant and realized that I was at once too early and too late with the Dessert Noir Café & Bar concept. I was on the front end of a big-city trend in the market toward dessert-focused restaurants and bars that was taking off in places like New York, Boston, San Diego, and Chicago. I was a pioneer and learned firsthand that it takes a while for urban trends and innovations to make their way to the suburbs. I brought the idea to the suburban market when the "natives" weren't quite ready for it.

In addition, by the time I opened Dessert Noir Café & Bar in January 2005, I had missed all of the big blockbuster movies and surprise hits that my business counted on to make its movie theater location a success. Movies like *The Passion of the Christ, Spiderman 2, Shrek 2, Ray, Million Dollar Baby, Super Size Me, Ocean's 12, Napoleon Dynamite,* and *The Incredibles,* to name a few. Little did I know that I'd suffer through more than two years of lackluster, not blockbuster, releases.

With that, I was forced to strongly consider the option of selling Dessert Noir Café & Bar much sooner than I wanted, and I was completely unprepared for the task in early 2007. Based on my initial financial projections and the promises of my upscale location and good demographics, I thought the business would absolutely be profitable by the time we reached the two-year mark in January 2007. At that point, we saw high-double-digit revenue improvement and a significant cut in our operational losses. Despite on-going positive press coverage, favorable reviews, critical acclaim, and customers who loved us, the business was taking too long to reach profitability and was losing too much money. The restaurant business pulls on customers' discretionary income, and in our case, that income was getting sapped in the wake of the sub-prime mortgage debacle in the housing and financial markets and increasing energy prices. The early costly "sins" that every entrepreneur endures to get a business up and running meant that I used essentially my entire cushion to cover the losses and continue to operate. I considered the emotional and financial stress that the business had placed on my peace of mind and my marriage, my two most important M Factors, and I realized that I was going to be dead or divorced before this experience was over. Neither option was good.

I focused on creating an "elegant exit," seeking to partner with a business broker to find the right buyer and continuing to operate Dessert Noir Café & Bar at the minimum amount of continued investment while improving the numbers to make the business more attractive to potential buyers. After months of searching, I was unable to find a single broker who would take my deal because of three significant factors: negative cash flow, high occupancy costs (rent and other landlord expenses) as a percentage of revenue, and location. As we moved into 2008, the tight credit markets didn't help my cause as potential buyers could not obtain the financing even if they were seriously considering doing the deal. Brokers and prospective buyers inevitably raised the same issues about lack of foot traffic and visibility that I had been struggling with for years and concluded, "Even after lots of publicity and marketing, Dessert Noir Café & Bar could not make it in this space and chances are we won't, either."

Well, why not simply go out of business with all of this working against me? Call me crazy but I saw a ray of light in this dark cloud. Here's what I considered:

It felt like it would take just as much energy, effort, and expense to go out of business as it did to start – e.g., informing and laying off staff, disposing of assets, untangling business relationships, notifying the press and government agencies, breaking contracts early and paying hefty penalties, settling debts, making final payments, and the list goes on. Most people who are in business with you want nothing more than for you to stay alive, even if that means weathering stormy periods, because you still represent revenue potential. If they know you're committed to making it happen, they'll likely hang in there with you.

It also helped that Dessert Noir Café & Bar happened to be located at a shopping center where the developer invested extremely large sums of money to create a vibrant retail destination. Empty spaces and stories of a business' demise would send exactly the opposite message. With all this in mind, I negotiated with my landlord and business partners to buy into my plan to continue to focus on making my business successful and negotiate on my obligations so I could eventually meet my financial commitments to them.

At the end of the day, perhaps it was the sheer force of my personality. I strongly believed that if I remained true to myself and my original vision, I could continue to gain more traction, get more recognition, increase sales, and find those breakthroughs along the way that would help the business stay viable. With this renewed focus on growing my business, I applied for Make Mine a Million $ Business, a program that Count Me In for Women's Economic Independence and American Express have developed to assist women entrepreneurs with growing their businesses into million-dollar enterprises. Women from around the country compete for business development packages that include money, marketing, mentoring, and technology assistance, and I was named a winner in the 2008 Pacific Northwest competition. (For more information about Make Mine a Million $ Business, check out the web site at www.makemineamillion.org.)

To demonstrate my commitment to my team, I focused on improving operational efficiencies and providing management training for my key players. To reach new customers, I partnered with a local restaurant delivery service to expand my dinner business and joined popular restaurant web sites that offer discounts and promotions for members to try local places. I took advantage of trade opportunities with local TV stations to expose their viewers to our restaurant and continued to cultivate my relationships with local reporters. I increased my profile on the local and national stage to become an advocate, spokesperson, and role model for small businesses and women entrepreneurs. Finally, as I described in Chapter 8, I still had a commitment from Morgan Freeman to come to town for a first-class fundraising event.

People other than me and my circle of friends, family, and supporters began to recognize that my business had the potential to succeed, and there was no way I was going to give that up. The rest, as they say, is history.

> ## Divas Lesson #10
> ### Every day your business is open is a day you defy the odds.

You've probably heard the statistic that "95 percent of all small businesses fail" and asked yourself, "How can this be true?" As I mentioned at the beginning of this book, data from the U.S. SBA show that two-thirds of new businesses survive at least two years, and about 44 percent survive at least four. U.S. SBA researchers note that these findings don't differ greatly by industry. No matter what market you're serving with your small business, you have about the same chances of survival as everyone else.

Women-owned businesses are the envy of the world right now. According to the Center for Women's Business Research, women in the United States own 10.1 million businesses, employ 13 million workers, and account for $1.9 trillion in sales as of 2008. In addition, three quarters of all women-owned businesses are majority-owned by women, meaning women control 51 percent or more. That's a total of 7.2 million firms. Women-owned companies comprise 40 percent of all privately-held firms.[19] As women business owners, our impact on this nation's economy is huge. We need to continue to be leaders and pioneers in entrepreneurship.

With that said, get open! Do your business and do it well. Be part of the 10 percent of our workforce who is directing the work of the 90 percent who are showing up for their jobs everyday. Make them deliver for you.

## LIVE YOUR DREAM.

DIVAS DOING BUSINESS

# ABOUT THE AUTHOR

M onique Hayward is President & CEO of Nouveau Connoisseurs Corporation, which she founded in April 2004 and owns and operates the award-winning Dessert Noir Café & Bar in Beaverton, Oregon. She is responsible for setting the company's strategic direction and managing its business priorities. Monique is also a senior marketing manager at Intel Corporation in Hillsboro, Oregon.

Monique is an entrepreneur and corporate player with 15 years of experience in marketing, communications, public relations, business development, and entrepreneurship. She has shared her knowledge and expertise as a contributing writer and interviewee for national and local television news shows (CNN's "Your World Today with Tony Harris," KATU Channel 2's "AM Northwest," KPTV Channel 12's "Good Day, Oregon"), web sites and blogs (Gaebler Ventures' online resources for entrepreneurs, WomenandBiz.com, BizChicksRule.com, Women Entrepreneurs – The Secrets of Success Blog), and print publications (*Oregonian, Phoenix Business Journal, Entrepreneur, Black Enterprise, Restaurant Startup & Growth*). She's also a frequent speaker at conferences and colleges and mentor to up-and-coming professionals and entrepreneurs.

Monique was selected as a winner in the 2008 Make Mine a Million $ Business program, a collaboration between Count Me In for Women's Economic Independence and OPEN from American Express that provides a combination of money, mentoring, marketing, and technology tools that women entrepreneurs need to help grow their businesses into million-dollar enterprises. She also was recently nominated for the *Portland Business Journal*'s "40 Under 40" award, which honors young business leaders and entrepreneurs in the Portland area. Monique also has worked as a commercial model and spokesperson and served as the executive producer, writer, and host of her own talk show on a local cable TV station.

A native of New York City who also spent part of her childhood in Columbia, S.C., Monique has a master of business administration in marketing from Case Western Reserve University and a bachelor of arts (*magna cum laude*, Phi Beta Kappa) in journalism from the University of Maryland College Park. She is an inaugural fellow of the ASCENT Mastering Management Program at the Tuck School of Business at Dartmouth College, participates as a visiting fellow for the Austin Entrepreneurship Program at Oregon State University, and teaches a course for aspiring women entrepreneurs at Portland Community College. She also is a member of the National Association of Female Executives and Entrepreneurs. Monique is married to Tom Freeman and the couple resides in Beaverton.

# ENDNOTES

1.  "Women Entrepreneurs ARE the Trend," by Sharon G. Hadary, *Enterprising Women: The Magazine for Women Business Owners,* Volume 5, Number 1 (2004), p. 22.

2.  "Businesses Owned by Women of Color Growing Faster Than All U.S. Firms," News Release from the Center for Business Women's Research, November 20, 2008, p. 1.

3.  "Business Employment Dynamics Data: Survival and Longevity, II," by Amy E. Knaup and Merissa C. Piazza, *Monthly Labor Review,* Volume 30, Number 9 (September 2007), pp. 3-10.

4.  "Are Male and Female Entrepreneurs Really That Different?," by Erin Kepler and Scott Shane, U.S. Small Business Administration Office of Advocacy Working Paper Research Summary, September 2007, p. 1.

5.  "Quotations by Oprah Winfrey," The Quotations Page Web Site. Source: *O Magazine.*

6.  "How Much It Takes to Start a Busine$$," CNNMoney.com, August 17, 2006.

7. "4 Ways Businesswomen Can Combat Bias," by Jeff Wuorio, Microsoft Small Business Center Web Site, Leadership & Training Section, 2008.

8. "Investment Bias Still Favors Male-Owned Firms, Despite Proven Success of Female CEOs," by Shula Neuman, *Discovery@Olin*, Spring 2006, Volume 5, Issue 2.

9. Women's Business Services, Wells Fargo Web Site.

10. Small Business Banking, Comerica Web Site.

11. "How Much It Takes to Start a Busine$$," CNNMoney.com, August 17, 2006.

12. "This is About YOU!," by Iyanla Vanzant. Keynote speech at Omega Institute and V-Day's Women & Power Conference, September 2004.

13. "Job Openings and Labor Turnover Survey Summary," U.S. Bureau of Labor Statistics, September 2008.

14. *Women Entrepreneurs: Turning Disadvantages into Advantages*, by Mai Nguyen, PreFlight Ventures, Inc., January 2005.

15. "The 16 MBTI (Myers-Briggs Type Indicator®) Types," Meyers-Briggs Foundation Web Site.

16. "Key Facts About Women-Owned Businesses," Center for Women's Business Research Web Site.

17. *Women Entrepreneurs: Turning Disadvantages into Advantages*, by Mai Nguyen, PreFlight Ventures, Inc., January 2005.

18. *Leaders in Business and Community: The Philanthropic Contributions of Women and Men Business Owners*, Center for Women's Business Research, November 2000.

19. "Key Facts About Women-Owned Businesses," Center for Women's Business Research Web Site.

# SAMPLE BUSINESS PLAN

As I described in Chapter 3, your business plan is your "holy book." As I prepared myself to write this plan for Dessert Noir Café & Bar, I consulted with other entrepreneurs, bankers, and potential investors as well as volunteers with the local office of the Small Business Administration's SCORE (Service Corps of Retired Executives) program and my community's local Small Business Development Center (SBDC). I also searched online for sample business plans and articles on tips and tricks for writing good plans. I literally got thousands of hits simply by doing a Google search on "how to write good business plans." There are more books than you can count on writing business plans, and two that I recommend are *Writing a Convincing Business Plan* by Arthur R. DeThomas and Lin Grensing-Pophal and *The Complete Book of Business Plans* by Joseph A. Covello and Brian J. Hazelgren.

What follows is my own original business plan. While I implemented the majority of what I conceived for my business, my vision was not perfect. Since launching my restaurant, I have updated the plan to capture changes to the strategy and implementation that have come with having real-world experience. For example, I originally planned for the restaurant to be open only for dinner, but within a month of opening, we added lunch hours. After three years of serving lunch, I went back to my original plan of being open only for dinner. It's always a work in progress.

Things to keep in mind as you're writing your plan:

## 1. Use simple, straightforward language.

I worked for a small marketing communications consulting firm many years ago, and the owner always advised his writers that the most powerful messages are delivered using simple, declarative sentences. Your business plan is not the document to demonstrate your expansive vocabulary or to write flowery, extensive prose.

## 2. Be brief.

The people reading your plan will be time-constrained and won't have the tolerance or the patience for a document that's more than 50 pages. Even then, they may not make it to the end and will likely only read the executive summary and review your numbers. As Polonius said in Shakespeare's *Hamlet*, "Brevity is the soul of wit."

## 3. Be realistic.

Ground your goals and objectives in the reality of your market and its growth potential. Prospective investors, advisors, and business partners will find your plan hard to believe if you're overly optimistic about your sales projections or you've underestimated the time and expense of launching your product or service.

# dessert Noir

## CAFÉ & BAR

## BUSINESS PLAN

**Author:**
*Monique Hayward*
Nouveau Connoisseurs Corporation
Address, Email, Phone
July 2004

# TABLE OF CONTENTS

Executive Summary

    Overview of Proposed Beaverton Dessert Café & Bar

    Target Market

    Competition

    Management

    Short-Term Objectives (Years 1-3)

    Long-Term Objectives (Beyond Year 3)

    Return on Investment and Restaurant Financials

    Risk Evaluation

Company Overview

Industry/Market Analysis

Venue's Concept

Target Market Analysis

Competitive Overview and Positioning

Sales and Marketing Strategy

Operations

Management and Key Staff

Financials

Appendices

# EXECUTIVE SUMMARY

## Overview of Dessert Noir Café & Bar

Scheduled to open in Fall 2004, Dessert Noir Café & Bar aims to be the premier after-dinner destination in Beaverton, Oregon, for middle-to-upper income adults. It will appeal directly to people who want a distinctive, sophisticated gathering place with great ambiance and "cool factor" that's close to home – a place where they can spend quality time during an evening out with friends, partners, significant others, husbands, and wives.

The venue will be approximately 2,000 square feet with a capacity of 60-70 people and will offer three distinct experiences for customers:

- **Café:** An experienced pastry chef will create high-quality desserts for customers who will be served in a chic and sophisticated, yet welcoming and comfortable, atmosphere. To build excitement and anticipation among customers, the dessert café will offer a lively, seasonally-driven menu of pastries, custards, cakes, pies, tarts, cookies, ice cream and sorbet. In addition to the pastry chef's signature creations, we will offer desserts from local, national, and international suppliers to round out our product offerings where necessary. We will focus on satisfying our customers' desire for familiar desserts as well as offering dessert temptations that stretch into the realm of adventure.

- **Counter Service/Bar:** A full-service bar will offer wine, beer, liquors, mixed drinks, innovative cocktails, specialty coffee, liqueurs, and cordials as well as non-alcoholic beverages such as coffee and espresso, hot chocolate, tea, soft drinks, and bottled water. The bar will feature limited counter seating for customers who choose not to sit at a table in the café. We will offer a bar menu of savory small plates and appetizers which will be served to bar and café customers alike.

- **Carry Out/Retail Shop:** A separate area will be designated for carry-out customers who order desserts and/or non-alcoholic drinks to go. This area also will be a small retail shop that carries gourmet food items (e.g., fine chocolates and candy, specialty coffees and teas, jams and spreads), specialty merchandise (e.g., coffee mugs, gift baskets), and wine (e.g., dessert wines, champagnes, ports, and other wines from Oregon and beyond).

To maintain a unique image of class and quality, Dessert Noir will provide attentive and friendly service. Management will invest in a formal training program for its employees to ensure its high standards for customer service are met.

After establishing these key elements of the evening-only business, we plan to offer customers the additional service option of using the space during the day for private events and parties (e.g., organizational and company meetings, small group celebrations, birthday parties, special events, weddings, bar mitzvahs, fundraisers). We will research the appeal of our holding our own special events and explore how these events could potentially enhance our concept. Possibilities include wine and dessert tastings in the carry-out retail space, dessert demonstrations and cooking classes, dessert buffet brunch, and live music in the bar/lounge area. We anticipate it will be at least six months after the operation is running before we will be in a position to offer these services. At that time, we will determine the potential demand, evaluate the feasibility in light of our primary business focus areas, and determine the product and service offering and pricing.

Dessert Noir Café & Bar will be located in Beaverton, Oregon, which is seven miles west of Portland in the Tualatin River Valley. Beaverton encompasses 15 square miles and is home to about 77,990 residents. It is Oregon's fifth largest city and is the largest incorporated city in Washington County. The on-going revitalization and redevelopment of the Beaverton area makes it a popular location and gives this venue a unique opportunity to thrive in a renewed business enclave with a mix of retail shops, restaurants, and local businesses.

# Target Market

Dessert Noir Café & Bar will target upper middle class/upper income men and women in the 25-44 age range who live in Beaverton and the surrounding area. Within this target audience, the venue will appeal to two primary market segments:

1. **Young Professionals:** The venue's location, approachable ambiance, and chic atmosphere will appeal strongly to young professionals who will find the venue perfect for casual yet sophisticated evening entertainment. Whether groups of friends or couples out on dates, this target desires convenient, happening dining establishments that deliver great food and excellent service.

2. **Suburban DINKs – Dual-Income/No Kids:** Upper-income, suburban couples and partners (married or not) without children who are time constrained will want an after-dinner destination without a lot of hassles that's close to home and will pay for convenience and superior customer service.

# The Competition

Dessert Noir Café & Bar will compete indirectly for every entertainment dollar spent in the area. However, the venue's direct competition lies mainly with two primary types of establishments: 1) Upscale formal or casual dining restaurants featuring a strong bar and dessert menu that are open beyond the normal dinner hour and 2) Traditional coffee, ice cream, and pastry shops with after-dinner hours.

# The Management

Dessert Noir Café & Bar will be owned and operated by Nouveau Connoisseurs Corporation, an Oregon S-corporation with the majority of the company's shares owned by Monique Hayward. Ms. Hayward will serve as the company's chief executive officer. She has over 10 years of business experience in the high-technology industry, specifically with Tektronix, Inc. and Intel Corp., and has managed significant programs in marketing communications, public relations, and business development. She has an MBA in marketing from Case Western Reserve University and a BA in journalism from the University of Maryland College Park.

GENERAL MANAGER BIO

EXECUTIVE CHEF BIO

## Short-Term Objectives (Years 1-3)

We have a unique opportunity to position Dessert Noir Café & Bar as the only venue of its kind in Beaverton and establish leadership in this high-end niche of the restaurant business. We plan to capitalize on an excellent location opportunity in a rapidly-expanding area of Beaverton and create an atmosphere and ambiance that "transports" customers to another place, where upon immediately entering the venue, they forget they're in "suburbia."

The objectives for the first three years of operation are:

- Create an after-dinner destination that provides guests with a unique eating and drinking option in the west-side suburbs and delivers outstanding food and attentive service that exceeds customers' expectations every time

- Launch the venue with a grand opening event for investors, business partners, employees, early customers, select members of the media, and supporters on or before February 1, 2005 (target Fall 2004)

- Maintain tight control of costs and cash flow through diligent management and automated computer control

- Manage the business within industry norms for costs as a percentage of revenue

    - Food cost below 33% of food revenue

    - Beverage cost below 25% of beverage revenue

    - Labor cost below 30% of revenue

The keys to success in achieving our objectives are:

- Locating the venue in a highly-visible, high-traffic retail environment
- Securing and maintaining the appropriate liquor licenses through the Oregon Liquor Control Commission (OLCC)
- Providing the combination of "cool factor," great desserts and drinks, ambiance, and exceptional service that creates a buzz, leaves customers with a long-lasting impression, and encourages repeat visits
- Building personal relationships with customers
- Staying on top of market trends (e.g., latest health and fitness fads, dietary considerations for customers with special requirements like low-fat, vegan, and sugar-free dessert choices), regulatory issues, and changes in demographics, customer tastes, and competition
- Maintaining high standards of quality, consistency, and reliability in all aspects of the venue's operations and interactions with customers
- Managing internal finances and cash flow to enable capital growth and implementing strict cost controls

## Long-Term Objectives (Beyond Year 3)

With the success and sustained profitability of the proposed Beaverton location, Dessert Noir Café & Bar will be established and will have potential for expansion to other Portland-area suburbs at the end of Year 3. We plan to investigate Lake Oswego, Tigard, and Wilsonville as possible targets for one new location. In Year 5, we plan to determine the feasibility of expanding the concept to other Pacific Northwest metropolitan areas, like Seattle-Tacoma, Washington. We intend to be extremely careful and deliberate about ensuring that business and market conditions and our company's long-term viability will allow for additional locations.

With two profitable locations and plans to expand the business beyond the Portland area by the end of Year 5, Nouveau Connoisseurs

Corporation will be well-positioned to take advantage of two possible paths that will determine the company's future. The first is to continue to invest in the company and diversify into related businesses. Some preliminary ideas include an upscale Portland nightclub and a suburban wine/cigar bar. The second is to exit the business by selling the dessert cafés. Potential buyers could include a larger company with local, regional, and/or national bakeries and cafés and would consider these venues to be complementary additions to its portfolio or a restaurateur looking for an established turn-key operation. At this point, management intends to pursue the first path and establish Nouveau Connoisseurs Corporation as an on-going concern.

## Return on Investment and Restaurant Financials

Preliminary financial projections for Dessert Noir Café & Bar indicate the restaurant will have sales of approximately $XXX,XXX annually at the end of Year 3, with $XX,XXX in projected net income. For investors, this suggests potential return on investment (ROI) of X% and return on equity (ROE) of approximately Y% by the end of Year 3. These projections are aligned with expectations in the restaurant industry in general.

The total cost to launch the venue will be $XXX,XXX. The start-up capital will be contributed from the following sources:

- $X from Monique Hayward
- $Y from business bank loan personally guaranteed by Monique Hayward
- $Z from personal contacts, family, friends, and investors

## Risk Evaluation

Restaurants are notorious for their high failure rates, but the conventional wisdom that 90 percent of restaurants are out of business in the first year of operation is not true. In 1991, hospitality professors at Cornell University and Michigan State University commenced a study of restaurants in three local markets over a 10-year period. Their study concluded the following:

| By the End of... | Failure Rate |
| --- | --- |
| 1 Year | 27% |
| 3 Years | 50% |
| 5 Years | 60% |
| 10 Years | 70% |

A more recent longitudinal study of restaurants in Columbus, Ohio, from H.G. Parsa, an associate professor of hospitality management at Ohio State University, found the failure rate was 57 to 61 percent for a three-year period (1996-1999). In addition to his primary research, Parsa's review of other published studies suggest restaurant failure rates to be closer to 60 percent or less after three to five years.

When compared with other types of small businesses, restaurants fare only slightly worse. According to the U.S. Small Business Administration, 66 percent of new employers survive two years or more, 50 percent survive four years or more, and 40 percent survive six years or more.

Unfortunately, the perception of the 90-percent failure rate lives on, and convincing potential investors and lenders that we have a good chance of success will be a challenge. We are addressing the risks of starting up this venture with a strong appreciation for ensuring the fundamentals are solid. In the table below, we have outlined a risk-mitigation plan to address the top issues that lead to failure in the restaurant business.

*Top Reasons for Restaurant Failure (Source: CapForge, Inc.)*

| Risk Factor | Our Plan |
|---|---|
| Poor Management | • Manager with extensive experience, knowledge of restaurant operations, and ownership stake in the business<br><br>• On-going review of management performance and effectiveness<br><br>• Implementation of automated systems to monitor and control costs – inventory management, order placement and delivery, point-of-sale, labor scheduling and tracking<br><br>• On-going monitoring of finances with quarterly reviews with board of directors<br><br>• Excellent hiring and retention practices to attract the best people<br><br>• Reward and recognition program to highlight employees' accomplishments<br><br>• Development and distribution of employee handbook, accompanied by employee training, to communicate policies and procedures<br><br>• Organizational culture where violations will be promptly disciplined, up to and including termination where necessary<br><br>• Opportunities for employee's on-going training and personal development<br><br>• Strict adherence to government health and safety regulations and restaurant food quality and customer service standards |
| Lack of Financial Resources | • Careful and thorough financial planning with conservative projections about revenues, costs, and profits<br><br>• Launch of venture only when enough capital has been raised to ensure start-up expenses are covered with a "cushion" for unexpected and/or last-minute issues |

| Risk Factor | Our Plan |
| --- | --- |
| Poor Service | • Conduct frequent employee training and education sessions employees regularly on best-in-class restaurant service practices<br><br>• Menu offerings and prices aligned with customers' expectations<br><br>• Measurement of customer satisfaction on a regular basis |
| Poor Market Analysis | • Complete assessment of market opportunity, including testing concepts and menu offerings with target customers<br><br>• Careful selection of location<br><br>• Effective marketing plan to reach target customers efficiently |
| Excessive Costs | • Strict cost controls and cash flow management<br><br>• Avoidance of "spare-no-expense" mentality and careful evaluation of spending decisions in the context of business objectives |

# COMPANY OVERVIEW

**Name of Company:** Nouveau Connoisseurs Corporation

**Name of Business:** Dessert Noir Café & Bar

**Business Description:** An after-dinner café and bar specializing in desserts

**Form of Business:** S-Corporation

**Owner:** Monique Hayward

**General Manager:** NAME

**Target Grand Opening Date:** November 2004

**Business Operation:**

Café and Bar:
3:00 PM to 11:00 PM, Monday through Wednesday
3:00 PM to 12:00 Midnight, Thursday, Friday, and Saturday
3:00 PM to 9:00 PM, Sunday

Carry-Out/Retail:
1:00 PM to close, Sunday through Saturday
Closed major holidays (New Year's Day, Memorial Day, Independence Day, Thanksgiving Day, Christmas Day)

**Location:** Negotiations in progress with C.E. John Co. for Cedar Hills Crossing, an upscale retail center located in Beaverton, Oregon

**Contact Information:**
Monique Hayward
Address, Phone, Email

**Business Advisors:**

- Chef/Owner, Restaurant in Portland
- Wine Steward, Restaurant in Portland
- Director of Operations, Fast Food Franchise in Portland
- Counselor, Small Business Development Center, Beaverton
- Counselor, Service Corps of Retired Executives, Portland
- Certified Public Accountant, Oregon City
- Attorney, Beaverton

# INDUSTRY/MARKET ANALYSIS

## Restaurant Industry Overview

The general economic climate in the United States is improving after two years of recession, which means good news for the restaurant industry, whose economic impact reached $1 trillion in 2002. This included sales in related industries such as agriculture, transportation, wholesale trade, and food manufac-turing. For Oregon specifically, that figure topped $9 billion.

| Economic Indicator | Overall U.S. Industry | Oregon |
|---|---|---|
| Annual Sales (2003) | $426.1 billion – on average, $1.2 billion on a typical day | $4.3 billion |
| Locations | 858,000 — more than 54 billion meals eaten in restaurants and school and work cafeterias | Over 8,900 – more than one of three retail establishments are eating and drinking establishments |
| Employees | Nearly 12 million — more than eight percent of those employed in the United States, which makes the restaurant industry the largest employer besides the U.S. government | 107,000 – Oregon's top private-sector employer |
| Restaurant-Industry Share of Food Dollar | 45.8 percent | 46 percent |

*Source: National Restaurant Association and Oregon Restaurant Association*

In 2001, the average annual household expenditure for food away from home was $2,030, or $812 per person. In 2001, almost half of all adults (44 percent) were restaurant patrons on a typical day. The typical person (aged 8 and older) consumes an average of 4.2 meals prepared away from home per week.

## Full-Service Restaurants:

The restaurant industry registered its 11th consecutive year of real sales growth in 2002, and with brighter economic prospects ahead, a majority of full-service restaurant operators expected business to get even better in 2003. According to the National Restaurant Association's 2002 Table Service Operator Survey, approximately three out of five full-service restaurant operators expected business to be better in 2003 than it was in 2002. About a third of full-service operators expected business to be about the same as it was in 2002, while less than one out of 10 operators expected a downturn in business. Operators of higher-check establishments were the most optimistic, with roughly two-thirds of operators with average per-person checks of $15 or more expecting their business to improve in 2003.

## Beaverton – A Strong Suburban Community:

Located in the heart of Washington County's famous "Silicon Forest" and only seven miles west of downtown Portland, Beaverton is the hub of a prosperous economic region, according to the Beaverton Chamber of Commerce. As Oregon's fifth-largest community and Portland's second-largest suburb, Beaverton attracts residents who enjoy the energy of a thriving city but prefer a hometown atmosphere and a strong sense of community. Residents enjoy excellent schools, a healthy business climate, attractive housing, and limitless opportunities for cultural activities, entertainment and recreation. Beaverton's proximity to towering mountains, scenic rivers and a dramatic coastline make it an ideal place to live, work and play.

We are targeting Central Beaverton, specifically Cedar Hills Crossing retail center, for the venue's location. This area's fast-growing residential and commercial base, accessibility by car and public transportation, and high incomes have made them highly desired locations for retailers, restaurateurs, franchise operators, and professional services firms.

According to February 2004 business license data from the City of Beaverton, there are 859 retail restaurants in the city employing 7,795 people. A rough calculation of market size for restaurants in Beaverton, Oregon, based on the average yearly expenditure for food away from home and the size of the population is approximately $63M/year. The target customer for our proposed business comprises about 35 percent of the population, meaning that the opportunity for restaurants going after this market is about $22M/year.

No one area in Beaverton has a large concentration of restaurants (like a "Restaurant Row") that many suburban cities have established. Diners in Beaverton will find restaurants in large and small shopping centers, strip malls along major thoroughfares, and tucked into corners of the city's neighborhoods. Listed below are descriptions and examples of the types of restaurants found in Beaverton:

| Category | Description | Examples in Beaverton |
|---|---|---|
| Locally Operated Bars and Lounges | Establishments appealing to local neighborhood clientele; same client base dictates average price structure be drastically scaled down in order to create "regulars"; emerging category of specialty wine and cocktail bars | Restaurant Names |
| Conventional Dining | Restaurants owned by large national/regional chains and occupy less than 10,000 sq. ft.; focus on serving good quality food at fair prices in a reasonable amount of time; superior to fast food, but still formulaic to allow easy duplication in multiple locations; often caters to families | Restaurant Names |

| Category | Description | Examples in Beaverton |
|----------|-------------|------------------------|
| Formal Dining | Restaurants specializing in high-quality food and superior service to deliver a unique experience for the customer; generally locally owned, often the subject of magazine and newspaper restaurant reviews, feature well-known chefs active on the "foodie scene," and can count on a regular following | Restaurant Names |
| Casual Dining | Range from the quaint small cafe to the restaurant/bar combination; easy menus typically featuring soups, pastas, sandwiches, salads, and desserts | Restaurant Names |
| Ethnic Dining | Either formal or casual, these restaurants specialize in cuisine typically associated with a geographic region or culture | Restaurant Names |
| Fast Food | Quick, cheap, and readily available alternatives to home cooking; convenient, economical for busy lifestyles, but typically high in calories, fat, sugar, and salt | Restaurant Names |

# THE VENUE'S CONCEPT

Dessert Noir Café & Bar paves the way for a new dining experience, creating an eating and drinking establishment that aims to be the premier after-dinner destination in Beaverton for middle-to-upper class adults. It will appeal directly to people who want a distinctive, sophisticated gathering place with great ambiance and "cool factor" that's close to home – a place where they can spend quality time during an evening out with friends, partners, significant others, husbands, and wives. The venue also will cater to the upscale customers' desire for a higher level of indulgence and sophistication beyond what's currently available in Beaverton.

Unlike other nightspots, this venue will focus exclusively on high-quality food and drinks delivered with outstanding and attentive service that exceeds customers' expectations every time. To maintain a unique image of class and quality, the venue will provide attentive and friendly service. Management will invest in training and supervision of its employees to ensure its high standards for customer service are met.

## Key Elements

Dessert Noir Café & Bar will be a full-service restaurant, where customers are seated at a table and place an order from a menu with wait staff. From a pricing point of view, we are targeting the average check to be approximately $17.00/person (food and drinks, excluding tip; please see Appendix A for sample menus).

The venue will be approximately 2,000 square feet with a capacity of 60-70 people and offer three distinct experiences for customers:

- **Café:** An experienced pastry chef will create high-quality desserts for customers, be served in a chic and sophisticated, yet welcoming and comfortable, atmosphere. To build excitement and anticipation among customers, the dessert café will offer a lively, seasonally-driven menu of pastries, custards, cakes, pies, tarts, cookies, ice cream and sorbet. In addition to the pastry chef's signature creations, we will offer desserts from local, national, and international suppliers to round out our product offerings where necessary. We will focus on satisfying our customers' desire for familiar desserts as well as offering dessert temptations that stretch into the realm of adventure.

- **Counter Service/Bar:** A full-service bar will offer wine, beer, liquors, mixed drinks, innovative cocktails, specialty coffee, liqueurs, and cordials as well as non-alcoholic beverages such as coffee and espresso, hot chocolate, tea, soft drinks, and bottled water. The bar will feature limited counter seating for customers who choose not to sit at a table in the café. We will offer a bar menu of savory small plates and appetizers which will be served to bar and café customers alike.

- **Carry Out/Retail Shop:** A separate area will be designated for carry-out customers who order desserts and/or non-alcoholic drinks to go. This area also will be a small retail shop that carries gourmet food items (e.g., fine chocolates and candy, specialty coffees and teas, jams and spreads), specialty merchandise (e.g., coffee mugs, gift baskets), and wine (e.g., dessert wines, champagnes, ports, and other wines from Oregon and beyond).

After establishing these key elements of the evening-only business, we plan to offer customers the additional service option of using the space during the day for private events and parties (e.g., organizational and company meetings, small group celebrations, birthday parties, special events, weddings, bar mitzvahs, fundraisers). We will research the appeal of holding our own special events and explore how these events could potentially enhance our concept. Possibilities include wine and dessert tastings in the carry-out retail space, dessert demonstrations and cooking classes, dessert buffet brunch, and live music in the bar/lounge area. We anticipate it will be at least six months after the operation is running before we will be in a position to offer these services. At that time, we will determine the potential demand, evaluate the feasibility in light of our primary business focus areas, and determine the product and service offering and pricing.

# TARGET MARKET ANALYSIS

Dessert Noir Café & Bar will target upper middle and upper income men and women in the 25-44 age range who live in Beaverton, Oregon. According to the most recent consumer expenditure report distributed by the U.S. Bureau of Labor Statistics, consumers in this age range are above-average spenders on food away from home, alcoholic beverages, and entertainment. Within this target audience, the restaurant venue will appeal to two primary market segments:

1. **Young Professionals:** The venue's location, approachable ambiance, and chic atmosphere will appeal strongly to young professionals, particularly women, who will find the venue perfect for casual yet sophisticated evening entertainment. Whether gathering in groups or as couples out on dates, this target market desires convenient, happening dining establishments that deliver great food and excellent service.

2. **Suburban DINKs (Dual-Income/No Kids):** Upper-income, suburban couples and partners (married or not) without children who are time constrained will want an after-dinner destination that's close to home and easy to get to. They appreciate the convenience of a suburban destination and are willing to pay for superior customer service.

Demographic statistics for the target audience are included below:

## Beaverton, Oregon

| Exhibit A | |
| --- | --- |
| *Total Population, Age 25-44* | |
| 25 to 34 years | 14,028 |
| 35 to 44 years | 12,739 |
| TOTAL | 26,767 |
| % of Total Population | 35% |

| Exhibit B | |
| --- | --- |
| *Married Couples as % of All Families* | |
| % Married Couples | ~80% |

| Exhibit C | |
| --- | --- |
| *Household Income, 1999 Dollars* *Income Above $50,000/year* | |
| Total Households | 14,877 |

| Exhibit D | |
| --- | --- |
| *Occupation (Employed Civilian 16+)* | |
| Mgmt., Prof. and Related | 17,719 |

| Exhibit E | |
| --- | --- |
| *Median Household Income, 1999 Dollars* | |
| Median Income | $47,863 |

*Source for Exhibits A-E: US Bureau of Census, 2000, Beaverton, Oregon*

## Upscale Formal or Casual Dining with Strong Bar and Dessert Menu

| Name & Location | Hours | Competitive Assessment (SWOT) |
|---|---|---|
| Restaurant #1 | Sun-Mon 11:30AM-9:00PM<br><br>Tues-Sat 11:30AM-10:00PM | S: Successful location at shopping center and probably its busiest tenant; strong use of menus for promoting upcoming events, specials, charity/community activities, etc.; wide variety of food in sizable portions – appetizers, sandwiches, pizzas, soups, salads, entrees (meat, poultry, seafood), pastas, desserts; bar offers full selection of house cocktails, wine, beer, liquor; great execution of "beach" theme; friendly staff<br><br>W: Some menu items border on "creative," but vast majority are unimaginative and appeal to the "mass market"; can be noisy even when there are not a lot of people; service can be uneven and slow; no dessert wines or ports on menu<br><br>O: Differentiate with better food quality, service, and ambiance for about the same price<br><br>T: Head-to-head competition for customers and could easily outspend us; could place greater emphasis on appetizers and desserts and expand offering |

| Name & Location | Hours | Competitive Assessment (SWOT) |
|---|---|---|
| Restaurant #2 | Mon-Fri 11:15AM-10:00PM<br><br>Sat 5:00-10:00PM<br><br>Sun 5:00-9:00PM | S: Long established; only restaurant of its kind in downtown Beaverton; bar attracts after-work crowd from surrounding high-tech, gov't, and local businesses; good service; solid menu with good desserts, wine list, and cocktails that are inventive/creative without pushing the envelope<br><br>W: Service and food quality can be uneven; long waits for bar tables during happy hour; desserts ordinary -- key lime pie, crème brulee, chocolate caramel brownie sundae, three-berry cobbler, butterscotch pudding, apple pie, and chocolate mousse<br><br>O: Establish venue as another choice for after-work crowd, particularly appealing to customers looking for non-smoking<br><br>T: Potentially revise dessert menu to include more upscale choices |
| Restaurant #3 | Mon-Thu 11:30AM-11:00PM<br><br>Fri 11:30AM-Midnight<br><br>Sat 8:30AM-Midnight<br><br>Sun 8:30AM-10:00PM | S: Good location in relatively new shopping center; modern, cozy, inviting with nice deco/design and layout; friendly, attentive service; broad menu with range of appetizers, salads, sandwiches, pasta; bar carries reasonable variety of beer , spirits, cocktails<br><br>W: Middle-of-the-road selections that neither offend nor excite; cocktails include inventive drinks, but nothing original; ordinary desserts – NY cheesecake, bread pudding, hot fudge brownie tower, root beer float, ice cream, vanilla bean crème brulee, chocolate mousse – appear to be an afterthought and are priced out of synch with rest of menu (3.25 to 4.75); limited wine list and NO dessert wines, ports, etc.<br><br>O: Feature upscale menu with more interesting, adventurous appetizers, desserts<br><br>T: Rework cocktail, wine lists to be more creative, feature desserts more prominently |

| Name & Location | Hours | Competitive Assessment (SWOT) |
|---|---|---|
| Restaurant #4 | Mon-Thu 4:00-11:00PM<br><br>Fri-Sat 4:00PM-2:00AM<br><br>Sun 10:00AM-10:00PM | S: New Italian cuisine that's casual, elegant, simple; sophisticated interpretation of traditional classics, regional specialties; fresh seasonal ingredients from local growers; upscale atmosphere with nice décor and ambiance; nice plating; good happy hour menu; full bar with some specialty cocktails<br><br>W: Flavors can be too intense (e.g., balsamic vinegar); positions itself as a place with "a touch of downtown quality cuisine and style brought to the 'burbs," which means higher prices than you find in suburban market; small dessert menu interprets Italian classics (tiramisu, amaretto bread pudding, trio of sorbets), obligatory chocolate cake (warm chocolate lava cake with vanilla ice cream), and seasonal items (hot apple pie in puff pastry with caramel sauce and hazelnut crème anglaise)<br><br>O: Not confined to a regional cuisine, can offer a broader selection of appetizers, desserts and after-dinner drinks that are more interesting and creative; offer higher quality at comparable prices; if this venue doesn't succeed, space could be an option for our location<br><br>T: Potentially expand cocktail, appetizer, and dessert menus to offer more choices at various price points |

# Traditional Coffee, Ice Cream, and Pastry Shops with After-Dinner Hours

| Name & Location | Hours | Competitive Assessment (SWOT) |
|---|---|---|
| Shop #1 | Sun-Sat 11:00AM-10:00PM | S: Strong brands with nat'l and int'l reach; good locations; low prices; quick service; consistent product everywhere; synergy with shops, retail products for grocery stores |
| Shop #2 | Sun-Sat 11:00AM-10:00PM | W: Consistency suffers with aggressive expansion; service at some locations better than others; generally only a single product as core offering; slowly diversifying into adjacent areas to leverage core product; pastries aimed at morning customers; with few exceptions, not open very late |
| Shop #3 | Sun-Sat 5:30AM-Midnight (drive-thru 24 hrs.) | O: Capture customers who view venues as "dessert of last resort" and offer great service in an atmosphere that's warm and inviting rather than one that encourages people to eat and run |
| Shop #4 | Sun-Sat Varies | T: Increase hours to attract evening crowds; alcohol as an add-on business; source pastries/baked goods more appropriate for after dinner; continued expansion |
| Shop #5 | Mon-Thu 6:00AM-10:00PM Fri 6:00AM-11:00PM Sat 8:00AM-11:00PM Sun 8:00AM-7:00PM | S: Laser focus on outstanding chocolate delights; highly-rated, critically acclaimed, nationally known; wide selection for enjoyment at café as well as pre-packaged retail items; welcoming atmosphere with open space, clean lines, and good lighting; offers some pastry items

W: New Beaverton location competes directly against 24-hour coffee shop and nearby national-brand ice cream shops; too much variation in consistency and quality of drinks

O: Offer range of dessert choices in better location for after-dinner crowd

T: Expand hours, offer more pastry items |

# SALES AND MARKETING STRATEGY

## Marketing Objectives, Strategies, and Tactics

In the long term, we aim to establish this new venue as the premier after-dinner destination in Beaverton for middle-to-upper class adults. With a thorough assessment of the competitive landscape, a unique position in the market, and a viable concept, we have determined that we can successfully promote the venue by focusing on the following marketing objectives, strategies, and tactics:

| Objective | Strategy | Tactics |
|---|---|---|
| Achieve 60-70 percent awareness of the venue among potential target customers in the first year of operation<br><br>Achieve 80-90 percent awareness of the venue among potential target customers in the second and third years of operation | Use local media, both paid and free, to get the word out, create buzz, and generate excitement for the venue | Advertising:<br>- Yellow Pages and directory listings<br>- Ads in Beaverton publications, *Oregonian* A&E<br>- Movie theater previews<br>- Restaurant listings in local newspapers, web sites<br>- Public radio traffic reports/sponsor breaks on OPB<br>- Highway 26 billboard<br><br>Public Relations:<br>- Grand opening event<br>- Press releases with invitations to local and select national food reporters/critics<br>- Press release to Alaska Airlines in-flight magazine ("Journal" section) and *Gourmet* magazine ("Road Food" column)<br>- Memberships in ORA, Hillsboro Chamber of Commerce<br>- Participation in charitable events and sponsorships<br><br>Web Site:<br>- Overview and contact info, news, menus, reservations, online ordering<br><br>Direct Mktg Campaign:<br>- Local businesses and residences |

| Objective | Strategy | Tactics |
|---|---|---|
| Make the target customers' list of top 5 preferred dessert destinations in Beaverton by the end of the second year of operation | Ensure the customer's experience at the venue meets or exceeds his/her expectations | **Seasonal Promotions:**<br>- Special, seasonal, and holiday dessert items throughout the year<br><br>**Monthly Specials:**<br>- Desserts of the Month, with wine/drink pairings<br>- Wine tastings with guest experts<br><br>**Customer Birthdays:**<br>- Free dessert on customer's b-day<br><br>**Dessert Club:**<br>- Frequent customer program<br><br>**Cross Promotions:**<br>- With other businesses |
| Establish the venue's brand with target customers by building an identity of high-quality indulgence and sophistication in the first year of operation | Deliver the venue's concept through creating and communicating an integrated and consistent look and feel across all aspects of the operation | **Common Graphical Elements:**<br>- Menus, brochures/literature, business cards, web site, photography and other communications vehicles<br><br>**Exterior and Interior Design:**<br>- Establish visual appeal, atmosphere, ambiance<br><br>**Employee Training:**<br>- Attitude, customer service, and operations procedures |

APPENDIX A: SAMPLE BUSINESS PLAN

# OPERATIONS

**Host/Hostess:** There are three major functions the host/hostess will serve. These include greeting, coordination, and seating. As the greeter, the host/hostess will greet customers immediately upon their arrival and escort them to their tables. As a coordinator, he or she will assist guests with expediting the seating process. The host/hostess then takes guests to their tables, introduces their server, and informs guests of the specials for the day.

The café will accept reservations by phone, on its web site, and at the venue. If the customer's table is not immediately available or he or she does not have a reservation, the customer's name will be placed on a waiting list and he/she will be invited to sit in a waiting area or the bar before being seated. At the counter at the bar, seating is available on a first-come, first-served basis.

**Service Staff:** At the café, customers place orders with wait staff. Customers seated at the bar can order drinks, appetizers, and dessert from the bartender. Customers in the carry-out section place their orders with and purchase their retail merchandise from the bartender.

**Food Production:** Signature dessert items and appetizers will be prepared on the premises. The wait staff may be required to put the finishing touches on items (e.g., simple assembly and presentation onto plates, heating, pouring sauces, adding ice cream or freshly whipped cream). The patisserie chef will determine the featured dessert of the month and the management staff will create other dessert specials.

**Cash Management:** The bartender will be assigned a register for the duration of his/her shift to maintain accountability. Upon opening, the cash drawer will have a balance of $300: five $20s, ten $10s, ten $5s, and fifty $1s. The drawer will be counted out after each major serving period, and discrepancies over +/- $1 will be addressed in the appropriate manner. Proper cash handling techniques will be taught to all staff handling money. Currency markers will be used on all $50 and $100 bills. The venue will accept cash, Visa, MasterCard, American Express, and travelers' checks. Personal checks will not be accepted.

Deposits will be made daily and change purchased at the same time. Management staff will make intermediate deposits throughout the evening when revenue exceeds $500. End-of-shift and end-of-day reconciliations will be made to ensure any discrepancies are immediately identified and resolved.

**Security:** We will take the security of our customers and staff seriously and will take steps to ensure our dessert café and bar is as secure as possible. All staff will be instructed in proper behavior strategies and tactics to employ during a robbery and will be educated on our restaurant policy in handling angry or aggressive customers. They will also be asked to alert management to any suspicious customer behavior that may present a possible threat. In addition, bartenders and servers will be trained on alcohol responsiveness.

It will be our standard policy to never let unknown persons into our establishment after hours and to not schedule staff to work in the restaurant alone at any time. The store will not open the back delivery door during non-delivery hours, and after dark two people will empty trash together. There will be a monitored alarm system. Money will be kept at all times in a fireproof safe except when being counted or in a register. Money will be counted in the office with the door locked.

**Vendors:** We have established relationships with these vendors to supply the following goods, supplies, and equipment:

| Category | Equipment/Supply Needs | Vendor Relationship |
|---|---|---|
| Food – Dry Goods | Flour, salt, sugar, baking powder, baking soda, chocolate, nuts, pasta | Vendor Name |
| Food – Dairy | Eggs, milk, cream, butter, cheese | Vendor Name |
| Food – Oils | Olive oil, vegetable oil, nut oils, shortening | Vendor Name |
| Food – Fresh | Fruits, vegetables, meats, bread | Vendor Name |
| Food – Can/Jar/Bag | Condiments, sauces, potato chips | Vendor Name |

| Category | Equipment/Supply Needs | Vendor Relationship |
|----------|------------------------|---------------------|
| Food – Pre-Packaged (for retail shop) | Chocolate bars, biscotti, specialty coffees and teas, jams and spreads, nuts, gift baskets | Vendor Name |
| Beverage – Wine and Beer | Wine, beer | Vendor Name |
| Beverage – Liquor | Spirits, liquor, cordials, liqueurs | Vendor Name |
| Beverage – Non-Alcoholic | Coffee, tea, soda, juice, bottled water (still and sparkling) | Vendor Name |
| Merchandise | Coffee mugs, cards, gift bags, books | Vendor Name |
| Equipment – Major Appliances | Reach-in refrigerators and freezers, convection ovens, 20-quart and 5-quart mixers, ice cream maker, hot plates, microwave, food processor, ice machine, dishwasher, 3-compartment and hand-washing sinks | Vendor Name |
| Equipment – Storage and Workspace | Display case, work tables, shelving, mats, ladder racks, storage bins and containers | Vendor Name |
| Equipment – Baking Supplies and Tools | Cake pans, spring form pans, sheet pans (18" x 26"), half-sheet pans (13" x 18"), cake extenders for sheet pans, mixing bowls, tartlet tins, ramekins or brulee dishes, molds, rings, whisks, ladles, spoons (wooden and metal slotted), rolling pins, knives (chef, serrated, and slicers), disposable pastry bags and tips, sauce bottles (squirt bottles), ice cream scoops, spatulas (rubber and offset), peelers, zesters, chinois, sifter, brulee torch, hotel pans (various sizes), cake rounds, cookie cutters, cutting boards, scales, pots, pans | Vendor Name |
| Equipment – Bar | Bar sinks, stools, ice bin, shelving, storage, glass washing system, dispensers, bar tools, mixers, shakers, liquor pourers, pitchers, mats, blenders, reach-in refrigerators, espresso machine, coffee maker, carafes, teapots | Vendor Name |

| Category | Equipment/Supply Needs | Vendor Relationship |
|---|---|---|
| Equipment – Serving | Dishes, flatware, glassware, condiment servers (salt/pepper shakers), bowls, cloth napkins, paper napkins, carry-out containers and bags, disposable flatware | Vendor Name |
| Equipment – Furniture/Décor | Tables, chairs, booths, interior décor (artwork, table toppers, etc.) | Vendor Name |
| Equipment – Point of Sale | POS system and training, cash registers, order pads, payment folders | Vendor Name |
| Maintenance and Cleaning – Supplies | Brooms, dustpans, mops, dishcloths, brushes, sponges, buckets, toilet bowl scrub brush, dusters, cleaning agents, sanitizers, soap, toilet paper, paper towels | Vendor Name |
| Maintenance and Cleaning – Insect/Pest Control | Extermination service | Vendor Name |
| Maintenance and Cleaning – Window Washing/ Janitorial | Window washing service, detailed cleaning | Vendor Name |
| Maintenance and Cleaning – Laundry | Napkins, bar towels, dish towels, laundry service | Vendor Name |
| Administrative - Office Equipment and Supplies | Personal computer, printer/fax, online and telephone services, desk, lamps, chairs, fireproof safe, filing cabinet, stereo system, CDs, office supplies | Vendor Name |
| Administrative – Clothing | Employee shirts, aprons | Vendor Name |
| Miscellaneous | TBD | Vendor Name |

**Staff:** Staffing for the dessert café and bar will include:

- One (1) general manager
- One (1) executive chef
- One (1) dining room supervisor
- One (1) pastry assistant
- One (1) host/hostess
- Two (2) bartenders
- One (1) kitchen assistant
- Five (5) servers

**Quality:** Given we are differentiating our venue on high quality and attentive customer service, we will be extremely dedicated to quality control. This will not only ensure a consistent customer experience in food taste and portioning, but it will also promote safe food handling and preparation and cost control. Our quality assurance plan consists of several important tasks:

- Daily visual and taste checks of the food being served
- Daily measurement and spot checking of portions being served, checked against sales figures for consistency
- Written portion and assembly instructions, used consistently by the café and bar staff
- Daily measurement and spot checking of refrigeration and freezer temps and storage conditions
- Consistent use of product rotation schedules, FIFO, and product receiving inspections prior to acceptance

The job of all staff and management will be to make sure customers receive the highest quality, correctly portioned meals that can possibly be delivered each and every time.

# MANAGEMENT AND KEY STAFF

**Owner:** Resume for Monique Hayward is included as Appendix B.

**General Manager:** Resume for General Manager is included as Appendix C.

**Executive Chef:** Resume for Executive Chef is included as Appendix D.

**Business Advisors:**

- Chef/Owner, Restaurant in Portland
- Wine Steward, Restaurant in Portland
- Director of Operations, Fast Food Franchise in Portland
- Counselor, Small Business Development Center, Beaverton
- Counselor, Service Corps of Retired Executives, Portland
- Certified Public Accountant, Oregon City
- Attorney, Beaverton

# FINANCIALS

**Included are the following:**

Cash Flow Projection – Year 1

Income Statement – Years 1-3

Start-Up Expenses

Additional supporting financials are available upon request.

# APPENDICES

Appendix A:  Dessert Noir Café & Bar Sample Menu

Appendix B:  Monique Hayward's Resume

Appendix C:  General Manager's Resume

Appendix D:  Executive Chef's Resume

DIVAS DOING BUSINESS

# MARKETING PLAN OUTLINE

To become the fearless self-promoter of your business that we discussed in Chapter 6, you need a marketing strategy and plan for execution. Here's a marketing plan template with the key components of your marketing strategy built in: market research, product, place, pricing, and promotion. If you need more coaching and insight as you're developing the marketing strategy for your business, try using these great resources. They cover all these aspects in more detail:

*Guerilla Marketing: Secrets for Making Big Profits From Your Small Business*
Jay Conrad Levinson

*Positioning: The Battle for Your Mind*
Al Ries and Jack Trout

*Entrepreneur Magazine's Ultimate Small Business Marketing Guide*
James Stephenson

*Duct Tape Marketing: The World's Most Practical Small Business Marketing Guide*
John Jantsch

# Market Research

**Target Market:** Describe the customers and the potential size of the market for your product or service:

- Who are they?
- Where do they live?
- What's their income level?
- What's their age range?
- What's their occupation?
- Are they married or single?
- Do they have kids?
- What's their lifestyle?
- What do they desire?
- What are their needs?
- What's their population?
- What are the key environmental and economic drivers for your customers in this market?

The U.S. Census Bureau, U.S. Bureau of Labor Statistics, local government agencies, chambers of commerce, and industry associations are great sources for this information.

**Competitive Analysis:** Describe your direct competitors. A simple model for competitive analysis is called "SWOT," which stands for "Strengths, Weaknesses, Opportunities, Threats." Analyze your competitors on each of these dimensions to determine where your product or service has advantages and what areas you may need to improve to surpass them.

# Product or Service

Describe the product or service you will deliver to your customers.

- What is the product or service category?
- What exactly is the product or service?

- How does it address a specific customer need or solve a problem?
- What is the value that you're delivering to your customers?
- What are your key points that differentiate you from your competitors?

When describing Dessert Noir Café & Bar in my marketing plan, I turned to the teachings of Geoffrey Moore, the well-known business and marketing consultant and author of the books *Crossing the Chasm* and *Inside the Tornado*, for guidance. To help define the product or service you're selling and describe it in a way that differentiates it from the competition, Moore advises using a simple template to construct the positioning statement for a product or service.

## Positioning Statement Template

**For** (target customers)

**Who want/need** (have the following problem or compelling reason to buy)

**The product/service** is a (describe the product or solution)

**That** provides (cite the key benefit)

**Unlike** (the competition),

**Our product/solution** (describe the key point of competitive differentiation)

## Sample Positioning Statement

For Dessert Noir Café & Bar, I created this positioning statement:

**For** middle-to-upper income adults who live in Beaverton, Oregon

**Who want** a distinctive, sophisticated neighborhood dining destination

**Dessert Noir Café & Bar** is a dessert-focused suburban restaurant

**That** provides the sense and sensibility of a downtown restaurant close to home

**Unlike** corporate-chain restaurants,

**Dessert Noir Café & Bar** focuses on high-quality handmade desserts, savory dishes, and specialty drinks delivered with outstanding and attentive service that exceeds customers' expectations every time

## Place/Distribution

Industry precedent, competitive considerations, customer buying behavior, and the type of product or service you're selling will help you define your distribution methods.

- Do you have a retail product that customers purchase from one or more outlets?
- Are you a wholesaler who sells to retailers and not directly to end users?
- Is your product best suited for catalogs, direct mail, or telemarketing?
- Will you sell over the Internet?
- Do you need a sales force?
- Are you selling a service that requires developing an entirely new distribution channel?

## Pricing

Knowing your target customers and where and how they'll buy your product or service as well as having clear positioning vis-à-vis your competitors will be critical to your pricing decisions.

- What is the demand for your product or service?
- How do price changes affect it?
- What are your costs and the desired profit margin?
- What is the competitive and legal environment and what constraints do they impose on you when determining your price?

- What is your pricing objective – e.g., profit maximization, quality leadership, revenue generation, cost recovery?

## Promotion

With a firm handle on your product, the value you will deliver to your customers, and a deep understanding of your unique position in the competitive landscape, you can develop a promotion strategy that will create visibility and generate demand for your product or service in the marketplace. Here I've outlined objectives, strategies, and tactics that focus on building awareness for your product or service, the most critical challenge you'll face as you attempt to establish your new business.

Feel free to modify this promotion plan based on the goals and objectives for your own business.

### *Sample Objectives, Strategies, and Tactics*

- Objective: Achieve X% awareness of my product or service among potential target customers in the first year.

- Strategy: Use local organizations and media to get the word out, create buzz, and generate excitement

- Tactics:

  o Pre-Launch "Teaser" Campaign

  - Join local business organizations and trade associations and attend networking events to expose yourself and your product/service to other entrepreneurs and prospective customers

    - Host a "Try Before You Buy" event for members to get a sneak peek of your product/service

    - Contact the editors of the organizations' publications to pitch a feature story on your product/service

- Get listed in organizations' directories for products/services

- Place "Coming Soon" flyers and brochures in the public areas of local business organizations' office buildings

- Identify local print and broadcast reporters who cover your industry and product/service category and send press releases and product samples for them to try and review

o Launch "Tell the World" Campaign

- Grand opening event or product launch party for customers and media with special activities and prize giveaways

- Create your own web site and use social networking tools like MySpace, Facebook, LinkedIn, and blogging to connect with customers online

- Direct mail with special offers to customers' homes or businesses

- Advertising

- Listings in online and print directories of local businesses

- Hire street marketing teams to hand out flyers and coupons

o Post-Launch "Sustain the Momentum" Campaign

- Create email distribution list for online newsletter

- Pitch local reporters on new developments and updates with your product or service

- Create special events

- Participate in industry conferences

- Sponsorships of events or organizations that align with your target customers and provide selling opportunities

- Charitable giving and community involvement

- Follow-up advertising and direct mail programs

- Joint-marketing with complementary businesses

• Results Tracking: Set a target and measure how you performed against it

o How many leads did you generate from the business organizations' events and meetings? Directory listings? Advertising? Direct Mail? Sponsorships?

o How many customers attended your special events?

o How many stories about your product/service appeared in the press?

o How many hits and visits did you get to your web site?

o How many people have you added to your email distribution list?

• Measurement: Conduct a survey of target customers to measure their awareness of the product or service at the end of the first year.

• Budget: Realistically plan and budget for all the costs of your promotions programs

o Create a list of priorities

o Keep an on-going "wish list" for programs you wish you could do if the money ever becomes available

www.ingramcontent.com/pod-product-compliance
Lightning Source LLC
Chambersburg PA
CBHW060548210326
41519CB00014B/3389